# Involving Parents:

A Handbook for
Participation in Schools

**The High/Scope Press**
High/Scope Educational Research Foundation

# Involving Parents:
## A Handbook for Participation in Schools

Peggy Lyons, Al Robbins
and Allen Smith
**System Development Corporation**

*This Handbook was produced as part of a contract between the U.S. Education Department and System Development Corporation. Points of view or opinions stated do not necessarily represent official U.S. Education Department position or policy.*

THE HIGH/SCOPE PRESS

Published by
THE HIGH/SCOPE PRESS
High/Scope Educational Research Foundation
600 North River Street
Ypsilanti, Michigan 48197
(313) 485-2000

**Library of Congress Cataloging in Publication Data**

Lyons, Peggy.
  Involving parents.

  "Studies and Evaluation Department, System
Development Corporation."
  "TM-6974-003/01."
  "March, 1982."
  Bibliography: p.
  1. Home and school—United States. 2. Parent-teacher
relationships. 3. Public relations—United States—Schools.
I. Robbins, Al. II. Smith, Allen. III. System Development
Corporation.

LC225.L98   ~~1983~~  1984   370.19'31'0973      83-12747

ISBN 0-931114-19-5

Printed in the United States of America

# Involving Parents
## Table of Contents

# Foreword

*"Involving Parents" is a thoroughly professional guide to effective parental involvement in school activities. It is a result of, and an accompanying volume to, the "Study of Parental Involvement in Four Federal Education Programs." The overall study was conducted from October 1978 through February 1982 by the System Development Corporation of Santa Monica, California, under contract with the U.S. Office of Education (now the U.S. Department of Education). The study produced several final reports and this handbook. The final reports are listed at the end of this section.*

*The following programs were examined in the overall study: Elementary and Secondary Education Act (ESEA) Title I, ESEA Title VII Bilingual Program, Follow Through Program and Emergency School Aid Act (ESAA). These programs were selected because they had formal requirements for parental involvement and differed in ways that could directly affect the quantity and quality of parental involvement.*

*Five functional areas of parental involvement were studied: project governance, instruction, non-instructional support, community-school relations and parent education. This handbook describes successful parental involvement practices in each of the five functional areas and presents implementation activities. A self-assessment manual and a resource guide are included in the handbook.*

## Methodology

Because of its breadth and complexity, the "Study of Parental Involvement in Four Federal Education Programs" was divided into three phases: the Federal Programs Survey, the Site Study and the Validation Study.

The Federal Programs Survey involved surveying representative samples of schools and districts associated with each of the programs. Across the four programs, personnel in 869 schools and 286 districts were interviewed by telephone in the 1978-79 school year. Information was gathered on parental participation in governance and instruction, and on the co-ordination of parental involvement.

The second phase was the Site Study. Across the four programs, 57 sites were intensively studied to determine the nature of parental involvement, factors influencing it, the outcomes, and the characteristics of participants and non-participants. Sites were selected from the Federal Programs Survey sample such that, within each program, a range of parental activity in governance and instruction was represented. Care was also taken to select both urban and rural sites and to find sites that differed in the number of federal programs present. Field researchers based in each locality received intensive training from the contractor, after which they spent four months observing project activities, examining documents and interviewing a wide range of people associated with the sites. The field researchers reported data to the contractor senior staff at frequent intervals. These data were analyzed in terms of completeness and validity. Where necessary, follow-up activities were assigned to the field researchers.

In the Validation Study, practitioner-oriented documents were prepared: a handbook of successful parental involvement practices that were found in the study; a self-assessment guide for districts and schools that want to evaluate their parental involvement activities; and a resource guide with information on where to find help when conducting parental involvement activities. The major effort in the Validation Study was an intensive review of these documents by school personnel and parents active in parental involvement activities. Their comments and suggestions were incorporated to make the final versions as useful as possible. Plans for the Validation Study originally included a tryout of the materials to determine what problems and effects accompanied the adoption of new parental involvement practices. This tryout was not possible because other program activities were given a higher priority.

Overall, the "Study of Parental Involvement" was not an evaluation of the various programs' adherence to regulations. At the time of data collection, the requirements for parental involvement in the various programs centered on electing a council and having meetings that involved consultation with the school or district. Confining the study to that activity alone would have ignored a body of research which indicates that parents are involved with schools in a variety of ways that can benefit their children.

However, the effects of regulation were included as part of the broader study. Also, program samples in the Site Study were chosen to represent a variety of contrasting circumstances so that the major emphasis of the study was on determining causality, not momentary program status. Thus, the study cast a wide net to examine all kinds of involvement with the hope of finding practices that districts and schools could utilize in order to improve their own educational offerings.

## Findings

The overall findings are presented here in two categories: project characteristics and general conclusions. Specific details about sites within the programs are available within the individual program reports.

## Project Characteristics

- Most projects had a project-level advisory group. Site study evidence showed that about one-third of the advisory groups made suggestions that were acted upon by project staff.
- A typical project for a federally funded program had an advisory group and scattered examples of other parental involvement activities. Few projects had no parental involvement, and few had extensive parental involvement.
- After advisory groups, the next most frequent form of parental involvement was as participants in communication with the project. Most communication was in written form and went from the project/school to the home.
- Projects often had parents serving as paid aides. However, in any one project there were very few parents serving in this role, and many were parents of children who were no longer part of the project.
- Most projects provided some form of parent education. Usually, this was in the form of a one-time offering.
- Many types of parental involvement activities occurred infrequently, including instructional volunteers, systematic programs for parents to teach their own children at home, non-instructional volunteers and face-to-face discussions among parents and staff.

## General Conclusions

- Projects that offered well-planned student services, that were well organized and that ran efficiently were also the ones where parents were most involved, and had the widest range of activities at the highest levels of participation.
- At projects where parental involvement flourished, there were observable benefits for students, parents and staff. There was no evidence of harm from parental involvement.
- Patterns of parental involvement were observed across the participating sites. This allowed identification of factors that strongly affected the quantity and quality of parental involvement.

## Discussion

Parental involvement activities seem to fall into two categories: effective and indifferent. Effective activities were characterized by active parents, well organized projects or tasks, and facilitating staff. Effective activities produced positive outcomes. Among the positive outcomes reported were:

- improved student attitudes, conduct and attendance;
- improved classroom performance when parents tutored students;

- better understanding of student needs;
- increased self-confidence and personal satisfaction for participating parents;
- active parental support of instructional program;
- augmented instructional resources.

Indifferent practices were the result of situations where parental involvement was viewed as a requirement rather than an opportunity. In these situations, parents were regarded as passive receivers, and parent advisory committees were often directly controlled by school personnel. These sites were not characterized by disaffection among parents and staff; most often there was the attitude on the part of both parents and staff that school personnel knew what they were doing and didn't want or need help from parents.

There were examples of beneficial practices in all areas within each of the programs. When sites with high-benefit practices were compared to sites lacking such practices, a pattern of activity and organization was evident. Seven critical practices were found in sites with effective parental involvement. They are:

1. **Provision of coordination for activities.** Effective parental involvement included scheduling, varied personal contacts and a knowledge of who could get the job done. Most of this coordination was provided by persons hired as parent coordinators, although coordination was sometimes provided successfully by administrative personnel such as principals. The attitude of the coordinator was critical: when the coordinator regarded parents as unqualified or as lesser folk, parents had negative attitudes toward any involvement. However, when the coordinator treated parents as concerned partners in the education of the child, many more positive attitudes and outcomes were noted.

2. **The assessment of needs and resources.** Much of this assessment was informal, but effective projects determined the needs of children or parents or schools and the efforts that parents could realistically contribute before beginning activities. This kind of assessment focused the energies of participants on solving problems and provided criteria for judging the success of activities. There were several instances of unsuccessful activities observed in the study. They happened when a staff member assumed there was a need and designed a program without consulting individuals who would be affected by the program.

3. **Specification and communication of parental roles.** This specification was important for both school staff and parents. For staff, the specification gave them a clear idea of what they could expect from the parent in a specific activity. Parents could clearly determine what

they would be expected to do if they participated. For many parents, interactions with school personnel had often been negative and they did not feel comfortable in school; a clear understanding of what they would be doing in school helped to allay discomfort. In instances where roles were not clear, confusion often led to misunderstanding between parents and staff.

4. **Recruitment, selection and assignment of parent participants.** Recruitment was most successful when it allowed the parent to talk to someone knowledgeable about what kind of association best suited the parent and the school. Assignment involved the matching of parents to specific staff. Schools and projects used a variety of methods ranging from the personal knowledge of the coordinator to the development of parent questionnaires to match parents with jobs and staff.

5. **Training of parents and staff.** When training provided participants with the specific skills, techniques and strategies needed to get the job done, much higher levels of success were evident. Not only the parents, but also teachers and other staff benefited from training that showed them the best ways to work with involved parents. When training was absent or minimal, much time was wasted with attendant frustration for both parents and staff.

6. **Establishment of communication channels.** This was most effective when it occurred at several levels and when it was a two-way process. Such communication enhanced problem-solving and was an important source of cross-fertilization. Without good communication, it was difficult to recruit parents and the benefits of parental expertise were not realized.

7. **Support of ongoing activities.** This included publicizing the benefits of parental involvement and recognizing individual parents with awards. Publicity and recognition helped to attract new parents and retain present participants. When such recognition was absent, parents felt that people did not appreciate what they were doing or that their contribution was meaningless. In both cases, parents tended to withdraw from involvement.

Common to all seven "vital ingredients" was the willingness to monitor and evaluate parental involvement activities. Such monitoring often led to improvements and better understanding, and the ability to react to changing needs and priorities. Methods included informal and formal surveys of parents and staff along with periodic meetings of participants to discuss ongoing activities.

There were no successful parental involvement programs when schools were not wholeheartedly committed to parental participation. However, there was evidence that when federal resources were made available and regulations specifically encouraged a variety of parental involvement activities, the frequency of beneficial parental involvement was increased. This was most evident, for example, in contrasts between the Follow Through Program and the three other programs. Most sites of the Follow Through Program, with its commitment to parental involvement as a central focus of the program, had more activities with greater benefits. In most sites of the other programs, however, parental involvement was viewed as a minor part of the project; only when local authorities committed local resources were there instances of high benefit activities.

In sum, it is clear that successful parental involvement requires good planning, careful organization and the commitment of school personnel. When these factors exist, benefits for children, parents and staff can be realized by having programs that involve parents in schools.

Gerald Burns
Project Officer
"Study of Parental Involvement
in Four Federal Education Programs"
U.S. Department of Education

# References

The following reports have been prepared from the "Study of Parental Involvement in Four Federal Education Programs."

Federal Programs Survey Phase:

*Parents and Federal Education Programs: Some Preliminary Findings from the Study of Parental Involvement.* (Keesling, 1980)

Site Study Phase:

*Parents and Federal Education Programs, Volume 1: The Nature and Consequences of Parental Involvement in Federal Education Programs.* (Dingler, Keesling, Lyons, Melaragno, Robbins, Sanders and Smith, 1981)

*Parents and Federal Education Programs, Volume 2: Summary of Program-Specific Findings.* (Keesling, Melaragno, Robbins and Smith, 1981)

*Parents and Federal Education Programs, Volume 3: ESAA.* (Robbins and Dingler, 1981)

*Parents and Federal Education Programs, Volume 4: Title VII.* (Cadena-Munoz and Keesling, 1981)

*Parents and Federal Education Programs, Volume 5: Follow Through.* (Smith and Nerenberg, 1981)

*Parents and Federal Education Programs, Volume 6: Title I* (Melaragno, Lyons and Sparks, 1981)

*Parents and Federal Education Programs, Volume 7: Methodologies Employed in the Study of Parental Involvement.* (Lee, Keesling and Melaragno, 1981)

Validation Phase:

*Involving Parents: A Handbook on Developing and Assessing Parental Involvement Activities.* (Lyons, Robbins and Smith, 1982)

# A Note on the Use of the Handbook

This handbook can be of benefit to any district or school that is interested in encouraging the involvement of parents. The ideas and suggestions described were found in local projects being carried out under the four federal education programs that were the focus of the "Study of Parental Involvement." *Despite having come from sites with federal programs, these ideas and suggestions are applicable to other schools or districts whose administrators want to involve parents in the educational process.* This is because the projects we studied engaged in a wide variety of activities, often going well beyond any literal interpretation of what was then the regulatory language of the federal programs. The handbook presents a comprehensive treatment of parental involvement.

The handbook is divided into three parts:

- Part I discusses the *how to's* of setting up parental involvement in home-school relations, school support, parent education, home-based instruction, instruction at school and advisory groups. It presents many strategies and practices that have worked in school districts throughout the country.
- Part II is a self-assessment manual (SAM) that enables a district to evaluate its present parental involvement activities and to plan improvements where they are needed.
- Part III is a guide that describes materials available to help organize parental involvement activities—forms, questionnaires, parent guidelines, etc. This guide also contains a section on procedures for identifying consultants who can provide training and technical assistance in the area of parental involvement.

To realize the maximum value from the handbook, *familiarize yourself with Part I first. Then, use those portions of SAM (Part II) that correspond to your district's parental involvement activities.* This will help you develop a plan of action, and will indicate which sections of Part I should be studied and which sections of the Resource Guide will be most profitable.

*Finally, to benefit from the suggestions in the handbook, a user will have to take into consideration all of the influences on a local educational program.* It has nearly become a cliché, but schools do not operate in a vacuum. Their programs are forged out of a complex relationship among state agencies, districts, the local community and sometimes the federal government. Further, schools operate under a variety of financial and other constraints that may differ widely from place to place. Thus, not all of the suggestions offered here are necessarily practical for implementation in every education program.

In summary, after you have considered carefully your local needs, desires and constraints, this handbook will provide you with a variety of ideas on how to reap the greatest benefits from parental involvement activities.

# Involving Parents:
# An Introduction

This Handbook . . .

- *is about involving parents in the educational process.*
- *is based on findings from a two-year study.*
- *is intended to be comprehensive, covering the complete range of parental involvement in schools.*
- *demonstrates that parental involvement is valuable.*
- *helps school districts measure the success of their parental involvement activities.*
- *is for parents, school staff and administators who want to set up meaningful activities for parents.*

## Parental Involvement in Education:
## Prospects for the Near Future

This handbook promotes the participation of parents in a variety of activities related to their children's education. Parental participation is of course not a new idea. Our democratic system is based on the principle that citizens should be involved in all aspects of government including education. Indeed, over the last 15 years, parental involvement has developed into a vital part of the fabric of public education in this country. This active participation of parents in educational affairs has been due in large measure to the influence of federal education programs instituted during the 1960s, some of which were the subjects for the "Study of Parental Involvement."

On the surface, the near future seems to promise a lessening of parental involvement in education. Many of those federal programs that played such an important role in the 1960s by requiring parental involvement have been cut drastically, eliminated entirely or folded into "block grants" awarded to states with little legislative direction.

Three factors, however, may result in a continuation of parental involvement in the schools. First, parents and school districts have become accustomed to parental involvement and have established many mechanisms to make it work. Second, with less and less federal assistance, school districts are turning increasingly to parents for support. And third, the move to decentralize federal programs may give local citizens the greatest say about educational projects.

This handbook is made for a world where parental involvement in education continues or increases. The practices described will be useful to state and local administrators and to parents who want to begin or improve upon parental involvement activities.

## Two-Year Study

In 1978, the System Development Corporation (a research firm in California) was contracted by the U.S. Office of Education to study parental involvement in grades K-6 in four federal education programs: Title I, Follow Through, Title VII Bilingual and the Emergency School Aid Act. SDC's charge was to find out what parental involvement was about and to describe ways that parents were involved in local projects. We also wanted to identify techniques used by staff and parents to make parental involvement a rewarding experience.

SDC first conducted a large survey of the four programs to discover the kinds of activities in which parents and projects were engaged. Then, field researchers watched 57 projects in action for about five months gathering information about each project's goals for parents and about the day-to-day involvement of parents in such activities as advisory groups, parent education programs, etc. We found many practices that appear to contribute to successful parental involvement. As a result, this handbook responds to many of the questions that practitioners have been asking about parental participation.

## Comprehensive Nature of the Handbook

During the study, local educators and parents described to us and showed us a wide variety of parental involvement activities. These activities include the full range of parental involvement that exists in the elementary school community at large. The activities fall into several categories:

- **Home-School Relations**—parents help to plan and carry out activities that stimulate the exchange of information and the building of trust between themselves and school staff.
- **School Support**—parents provide time, goods and services to the school to help support its activities.
- **Parent Education**—parents participate in school-sponsored workshop and training sessions designed to help them become better parents and more knowledgeable citizens.
- **Home-Based Instruction**—parents supplement and reinforce their children's learning by teaching them at home.

- **Instruction at School**—parents participate directly in the education of children by aiding teachers in the classroom.
- **Advisory Groups**—parents provide advice and consultation to staff during the process of decision making about how the district or school is to operate.

Each of these areas is treated at length in the handbook. Therefore, we believe our handbook offers not only breadth but depth. Best of all, the practices and strategies that are the heart of the book are based on the findings of the study. They are strong examples of what local educators are doing in the real world.

## Parental Involvement Has Value

Our handbook takes a definite point of view about parental involvement: *it is valuable.* We believe that schools which involve parents are better places because of that involvement. The findings from the study supported this belief. Districts that had meaningful parental involvement reported a number of benefits to the schools, to parents and, most importantly, to the children. For example:

- Children whose parents help them at home do better in school. Those whose parents participate in school activities are better behaved and more diligent in their efforts to learn.
- Teachers and principals who know parents by virtue of their participation in school activities treat those parents with greater respect. They also show more positive attitudes toward the children of involved parents.
- Administrators find out about parents' concerns and are thus in a position to respond to their needs.
- Parental involvement allows parents to influence and make a contribution to what may be one of their most time-consuming and absorbing tasks—the education of their children.

Benefits like these and the many others cited throughout the handbook make parental involvement well worth the effort.

## Success Can Be Measured

If schools want to give parents real opportunities for participation and benefit more from their participation, they need to set goals and assess performance. We suggest some standards that are based on actual practices observed at schools that chose to offer "meaningful participation" to parents. "Meaningful" can be interpreted many ways, depending on the area of potential involvement being discussed and the needs of the local district and schools. In Part I, what we believe can be considered success— and why—will be described for each area of involvement. SAM then takes these standards and helps you apply them to your district's operations.

## For Those Who Want Success

As we said, this handbook is ambitious—it helps you establish and achieve concrete goals for your district or school. We think the rewards of meaningful parental involvement make the effort worthwhile, but achieving success does require effort. Those who use this handbook must want to succeed. Wanting to succeed, however, is only the beginning. Creating effective parental involvement programs also requires knowing what to do.

During our study we saw several districts and schools where parental involvement was working well. Examining those places to determine why their activities were successful, we found that most of them had taken the same steps in planning and implementing parental involvement activities. We call these steps "vital ingredients" because they are critical to success regardless of what parental involvement activity is being developed. We identified seven "vital ingredients," or steps to take.

- Provide coordination for activities.
- Assess needs and resources.
- Specify and communicate parent roles.
- Recruit, select and assign parent participants.
- Train parents and staff.
- Establish communication channels.
- Support ongoing activities.

The "vital ingredients" are described in detail in Part I, Chapter 2, and reappear throughout the handbook.

## A Final Word

This handbook is written for the energetic. Some of the practices described involve changing habits, behaviors and attitudes, if they are to be implemented. The creation of conditions that lead to successful parental involvement in any area may also require a willingness to honestly evaluate present practices and a resolve to change them if they do not produce the desired results. In short, it takes hard work and genuine commitment to fashion meaningful parent involvement.

# PART I

## *How to Set Up Parental Involvement Activities*

# *How to Set Up Parental Involvement Activities*

*This part of the handbook describes all that we have learned about shaping parental involvement programs that work. It begins with a discussion of home-school relations (Chapter 1). Good relations between parents and the schools set the stage for a successful parental involvement program. The "vital ingredients" will be easier to implement if lines of communication are open between the home and school, and an atmosphere of mutual trust prevails. Chapter 2 describes the "vital ingredients": those seven steps that lie at the heart of promoting meaningful parental participation. Chapters 3-7 address the various ways that parents get involved in schools from offering non-instructional support to participating in advisory groups. These chapters are organized by "vital ingredients" and include examples of "What Works: Successful Practices" for each ingredient.*

*Part I is not designed to be read from the first page through to the last. While we encourage a user to read all of it, we recommend the following procedure to focus your efforts. **Read Chapters 1 and 2 before going on to any other chapter.** They are the foundation for all that follows. Then, select from Chapters 3 through 7 the activity areas you are most interested in and read the specific suggestions offered in those chapters.*

# Creating Positive Home-School Relationships

The handbook begins with this chapter for a very simple but very powerful reason: good relationships between parents and the school set the stage for successful parental involvement programs. Efforts at starting and improving parental involvement are greatly affected by the quality of home-school relationships—how well parents and school personnel are getting along. While our study demonstrated forcefully the importance of positive home-school relationships, it also revealed that these relationships do not happen automatically. Open communication and personal interaction among parents and school personnel are required to foster mutual trust and respect. In this chapter we first define positive home-school relationships. Then we explain why they are so important. Finally, we describe specific techniques that were effective for promoting home-school relationships in the study.

## What Are Positive Home-School Relationships?

The term, "home-school relationships," covers two types of interactions between schools and parents: information exchange and interpersonal relations.

**Effective information exchange is the open sharing of ideas and opinions, between parents and school staff, concerning issues of mutual concern.** When information flows freely from the school to the home, parents stay informed of school activities and schedules. When information flows freely from the home to the school,

school staff are aware of parents' concerns and desires. With an open exchange of information, parents and school staff are more likely to see each other as strong allies in education—as people working together and supporting one another to achieve common goals.

**Interpersonal relations refers to the face-to-face contact between parents and school staff.** Positive relations require that parents and school staff know each other on a personal basis, and are comfortable and candid as they work together on school-related matters. This does not mean that parents and school people must all become close friends. It does mean that both parents and staff are able to express their opinions without the fear of being misunderstood or causing antagonism.

Good interpersonal relations are especially important, and sometimes especially difficult, if staff and parents come from different economic or cultural backgrounds. In these cases, many parents may be reluctant to contact a large public institution like a school, and many staff members may feel that parents are uninterested or even hostile. Developing bridges in such situations is challenging, but the results are worth the effort.

## Why Are Positive Home-School Relationships Important for Parental Involvement?

Positive home-school relationships provide a solid foundation for the kinds of parental involvement we describe in the following chapters. More specifically, such relationships contribute greatly to the development of the seven "vital ingredients" for successful parental involvement. They do so in two ways:

- **Positive home-school relationships establish a favorable context for parental involvement activities.** Any parental involvement activity asks parents and school staff to expend time and energy. People will be more likely to participate if they already trust one another and believe, based on previous contact, that participation will be pleasant and rewarding.

- **Positive home-school relationships create a network of staff and parents that can be tapped to participate in an activity.** School staff will already know many of the parent leaders, and parents will already understand the concerns of the professionals.

In summary, the preparation of the "vital ingredients" for meaningful involvement in any activity area will be far easier if parents and school staff are already on good terms. People, after all, are more willing to work with people they know and respect than with strangers.

## What Is Necessary to Create Positive Home-School Relationships?

In the next section we present a number of specific techniques we found in the study that were used to promote positive home-school relationships. As you read these descriptions, keep in mind three key points.

- **It is important to try to reach all parents.** This can be achieved by using several techniques in combination, although the particular combination you use will depend on your resources and conditions.
- **The process must be two-way.** Some techniques produce contact that runs only one-way. For instance, fliers promote contact from school to home, while a hot line promotes contact from home to school. Effective relationships call for mutual contact and this is another reason for using techniques in combination.
- **It is important to provide active leadership.** There are few situations where parent-school teamwork develops without leadership. This point is so important, we need to devote some additional attention to it.

The principal of a school can take some of the leadership responsibility. The principal can include home-school activities in a regular newsletter and calendar, and can discuss home-school relationships at PTA meetings and school staff meetings. Parent volunteers can assume leadership by writing articles on home-school activities for the newsletter or by recruiting other parents for specific activities.

But principals have many other school responsibilities and can't devote all their time to parental involvement. Parent volunteers also may not have all the time that the leadership role requires. It is important, then, to have someone at the school whose main responsibility is fostering positive home-school relationships. This person oversees all efforts, planning and implementing the techniques described next in this chapter. This means having someone to make sure there are enough volunteers and resources for activities, and to gather information on how well activities are working.

In conclusion, your efforts to promote positive home-school relationships will be most effective if you see that there is *leadership* for the efforts, and use a variety of techniques to reach *all parents* and establish *two-way* interchanges.

# Techniques to Promote Information Exchange

## Home Contacts

Staff members visit the homes of parents to let them know about school services and parental involvement opportunities. In this capacity, school counselors and resource teachers can act as intermediaries between other school staff and parents. If appropriate, some of them should be bilingual, which will contribute to the positive reception they receive from parents. Phone calls can be used for these same purposes, especially if the school or district is large and staff members cannot visit all parents in their homes. (In these cases, home visits can be used for parents who have not responded to other attempts to contact them or who have children who need special services.)

## School Contacts

Parents can also be encouraged to visit the schools. For example, a "Parent Visitation Day," held twice a year, gives parents an opportunity to meet teachers and observe the classroom routine. An annual "Back to School Night" orients parents to classroom procedures and lets them see some of the materials that were used during the school year.

Parent-teacher conferences allow parents and teachers to meet each other on a one-to-one basis. These conferences are a means of informing parents about their children's progress and obtaining comments from parents. One method has teachers hold an individual session with each parent within the first six weeks of school and make follow-up phone calls through the remainder of the year, as needed. These sessions usually cover attendance, grades and discipline, and how the parents can assist their children.

Finally, meetings can be held at school for parents to discuss such topics as how the needs of the schools and community can be met through cooperative effort, and what special educational services are offered or could be offered by the schools. These topics can be covered as part of a PTA meeting or in a separate parent meeting. Often, it is helpful to hold meetings both at school and in various community locations to maximize parent turnout.

## Parent Library or Parent Room

Small districts can set aside space for a parent library at the district office; larger districts can arrange library-type rooms at each school. These libraries are always open to parents and contain resources that would not be appropriate to send to parents, such as grant applications, school documents and books on parenting and other topics.

Schools can also set aside a room where parent coordinators, parent aides and parent advisory group members work and spend some of their spare time. This room may also serve as the parent library. The parent room provides a casual setting where parents can visit with school staff and keep informed about school activities.

### Parent Survey

A parent survey is an excellent tool for gathering information from parents about their concerns, interest in their children's education and instructional issues. More specifically, the purposes of a parent survey are:

— *to determine what areas parents want to focus on in parent education;*
— *to find out what problems parents are having in helping their children with school work;*
— *to assess satisfaction with the teachers and the curriculum;*
— *to find out which home-school communications efforts are working and ask for suggestions on how to better inform parents about the schools.*

Parent surveys can be conducted yearly. A school can report the results in its newsletter. Or the school can report the results to its parent advisory group as part of the annual school evaluation. Parent surveys can also include assessments of needs and resources for certain types of parental involvement.

### Parent Hot Line

Schools set up a direct phone line to a school representative such as a counselor, teacher or parent coordinator. Parents can call any time about any problem and the representative follows up on the problem to try to get it resolved. A more limited approach, if necessary, is to set up the hot line for certain days of the week or certain times of the day.

### Written Communications from the Schools

Fliers are used, on a one-shot basis, to announce a special event or inform parents about an upcoming meeting. Fliers are not only sent home but are also posted on bulletin boards around the school, parent room and community buildings that parents are likely to visit. Local religious groups are often influential in close-knit communities. Recognizing this, schools may send fliers to religious leaders inviting the congregation to attend school functions. Yearly calendars of events are often sent to parents in the form of fliers.

Newsletters are used to provide information to parents on a regular basis. A newsletter can include the agenda for an upcoming meeting, the minutes of a past meeting or schedules of parent involvement activities. Contributions from the children, such as poems and drawings, may be published in English or other languages. A newsletter can be used to enhance multicultural understanding. It would include ideas for activities that parents could participate in with their children such as trips to museums and ethnic restaurants. In addition, recipes for different ethnic dishes are published.

### Parent Handbook

Produced annually and distributed to all parents, a handbook describes the history of the school or district, lists parent leaders and staff members and how they can be reached, and discusses some key topics in education, such as the way students are grouped for reading or the importance of homework. The handbook can also list meetings scheduled for the school year including particular opportunities for parent involvement. The parent handbook might provide information about community resources, religious organizations and libraries around town.

### Media Announcements

School news is often publicized through television, radio and newspapers. Parents who do not have an opportunity to read fliers and newsletters may be reached in these ways. In some communities, the school invites a local newspaper to cover school events and prepare stories on educational efforts at the schools. Newspapers may also include messages about upcoming school activities. Notably, the media can be valuable to schools that do not have adequate funds for other home-school communication efforts.

# Techniques to Promote Interpersonal Relations

### Luncheons and Dinners

Everyone can relate to food. Any activity that includes a meal and an invitation to the entire family will usually draw a large crowd. It provides a chance to eat and engage in recreation. The school might put on an annual luncheon for school staff and parents. The parent advisory group can sponsor an annual "Kick-Off Chili Break" in the fall, for parents and staff to eat and get acquainted. "Restaurant Day" can be held every Tuesday; each parent brings a dish and eats lunch along with the staff.

A potluck dinner for parents and staff is a good tool for promoting interpersonal relations at schools. Many of these gatherings present an opportunity to taste foods of different cultures. But they also allow parents and staff to mingle on an informal basis. In some schools potluck dinners include district administrators, community leaders and students, as well as parents and staff. Parents bring various dishes and the students provide entertainment. Local community leaders donate door prizes to be distributed at the dinner. Schools can hold similar potluck dinners, on a smaller scale, throughout the year in parents' homes.

These luncheons and dinners are also an opportunity to recognize parent leaders for their efforts to promote home-school relations and for their work in other functional areas of parental involvement.

### Parent and Staff Outings

Field trips can be arranged to provide parent education. But they also provide an opportunity for parents to get to know each other and school staff. The school can sponsor an annual, end-of-the-year retreat for all parents and staff. This gives both groups a chance to get away from the school, relax and relate to each other as people. These events may require special funding or schools may ask parents to bear at least part of the cost. But schools may also obtain full or partial support for these events from businesses, such as hotels, private campgrounds and restaurants.

### Multipurpose Events

An event designed to share information with parents can also include opportunities for chatting and socializing. Assemblies have proven to be an effective way to stimulate informal interaction between parents and staff. First, assemblies attract parents because their children are involved in the performances. Second, assemblies can be held in a social atmosphere. Refreshments can be served and parents can be invited to stay after the assembly to talk with each other and with staff members.

A "School Awareness Week" is another way to encourage parents to come to school, to meet each other and staff members. If activities are spread over an entire week, parents who are unable to come to school on a particular day can choose another day that fits better with their schedules.

## Some Last Words

Throughout this chapter we have said that positive home-school relationships are important. They are valuable in and of themselves. If a school managed to establish the information exchanges and healthy interpersonal relations described earlier, that school would have gone a long way toward achieving valuable parental involvement. But positive home-school relationships also are valuable for what they offer to other types of parental involvement. A situation in which information is exchanged freely and people relate well to one another will be fertile ground for the growth of the parental involvement activities described throughout the rest of the handbook.

# 2 The Vital Ingredients for Successful Parental Involvement

- *Provide coordination for activities.*
- *Assess needs and resources.*
- *Specify and communicate parent roles.*
- *Recruit, select and assign parent participants.*
- *Train parents and staff.*
- *Establish communication channels.*
- *Support ongoing activities.*

In the Study of Parental Involvement we had several districts and schools where parental involvement programs were working well. Examining these places to determine why their programs were successful, we found that most of them had taken a number of the same steps in planning and implementing parental involvement activities. We were able, through our analyses, to identify the core group of common steps and to explain how each contributed to the effectiveness of parental involvement.

As already noted, we call these steps "vital ingredients" because they are critical to "recipes" for success. In addition, the seven ingredients are important no matter what parental involvement activity is being developed. We have, therefore, made them the bedrock of our handbook.

This chapter presents an overview of the "vital ingredients," describing them and discussing briefly why they are important. We also offer some suggestions about things to keep in mind when you are preparing an ingredient for your program.

The seven "vital ingredients" will appear again in each of the following chapters where we discuss ways of involving parents in the school. In those chapters we recommend actual practices that have proved to be effective in satisfying the ingredients for a particular parental involvement area.

# A. Provide Coordination for Activities

In those districts and schools in our study where parental involvement activities were most widespread and successful, a major contributing factor was the work of an individual who had direct responsibility for developing and coordinating the activities. These individuals had a number of titles including parent coordinator, home-school liaison and parent involvement specialist. Some of them were specifically designated by a district or school to coordinate parental involvement activities; others assumed such responsibilities while actually fulfilling another full-time role.

We found that, by whatever title they were known, coordinators were important actors in organizing and pushing for parental involvement. They tended to play four kinds of roles in the schools, each of which helped parental involvement programs to function. As *facilitators,* coordinators performed duties that supported, promoted and made easier the participation of parents in various activities. As *providers of information,* they were at the hub of communications between home and school and among parents. School staff and parents both frequently relied on the coordinators to act as a liaison between the community and the school. Coordinators also were *administrators* of parental involvement activities performing such tasks as maintaining records of participating and non-participating parents and cataloging resources. Finally, coordinators served as *trainers* of participating parents both in workshop settings and on a one-to-one basis. Being knowledgeable both about community practices and school operations, coordinators were often effective in training parents in the skills needed to support the educational process.

If you look back now at the list of seven "vital ingredients" presented in the introduction to this chapter, you will see why we have placed "provide coordination" first on the list. *The individual (or individuals) assigned coordination responsibilities ought to play a key role in making certain that all of the other "vital ingredients" are satisfied.* Coordinators had a major hand in planning, organizing and sustaining the most successful parental involvement that we observed. They often conducted the assessment, role defining, recruitment, communication, training and support service activities that make up the handbook's "vital ingredients."

# B. Assess Needs and Resources

During the study, we saw several instances where districts had put together parental involvement activities without thinking seriously about the needs and desires of parents or school staff. Nearly as prevalent were districts that gave little attention to the resources available to carry out activities—resources such as having parents with the necessary skills or staff people with the necessary time. In these districts parental involvement suffered. On the other hand, parental involvement tended to thrive in those districts that acquired information about needs and resources before organizing new activities or designing changes in ongoing activities.

You will have to consider two basic questions as part of the assessment process. First, in what areas is parental participation needed? Second, which parents and staff can and will participate? Procedures built around these two questions should be aimed at parents, teachers and administrators, since each group will have to support and participate in the activities if success is to be achieved.

**Assessment of needs ensures that an activity serves a real purpose, either satisfying a clear need for a service or responding to a widespread interest.** Since most parents and staff have limited uncommitted time, an activity must be seen by them as critical to the functioning of the school's educational program or rewarding in itself for their interest to be sustained.

**Assessment of resources ensures that there are enough parents and staff to carry out an activity.** It also helps determine whether the appropriate facilities, training and support services can be provided.

Two types of assessments can be conducted to determine what needs to be done and who can do it. An *informal* assessment is one approach. This might involve observation over time or word-of-mouth. Informal assessment requires that the person doing the assessing has an open, honest relationship with parents and knowledge of school operations. We discovered that parent coordinators, because of their position between home and school, were significant contributors to informal assessments. For example, during home visits they often talked with parents about what they (the parents) wanted to learn in parent education classes.

Another assessment method is the *formal* one in which parents and staff are surveyed to learn their opinions about what parental involvement activities are needed and what skills or interests they may have to offer. Most formal assessments that we saw were conducted with a short questionnaire although there were some other mechanisms that will be introduced in the chapters to follow.

As you think about this "vital ingredient," keep two things in mind. First, either an informal or a formal assessment can be effective depending on the desired level of information. *More important than the method is that you tap both the needs and resources of parents and professional staff.* Second, build in some time to process this information once you have gathered it. Sorting through a variety of comments and opinions will undeniably take awhile but in the long run it will pay great dividends. Besides giving you a sound basis on which to plan useful and interesting activities, a needs and resources assessment will provide critical information for establishing roles for parents—the next "vital ingredient."

# C. Specify and Communicate Parent Roles

The assessment process will have helped you make decisions about the general shape of parental involvement activities. As more specific plans for activities are fashioned, you will need to define as clearly as possible the actual roles that parents are expected to take in district or school operations. We found in our work that decision makers often assumed that staff and parents understood the roles parents would play in the educational process. As a result, confusion and conflict arose as participants tried to implement appropriate activities. At sites where time was taken to develop a common understanding among administrators, teaching staff and parents about what parents would be doing to support the school, participants reported that activities tended to proceed smoothly and efficiently.

This "vital ingredient" requires that for each functional area in which parents are to be involved, policy statements about the depth and breadth of that involvement be developed and publicized. These statements will serve as blueprints for action. For example, many effective advisory groups draw up, in cooperation with district administrators, their own set of bylaws. That is not to say that such statements should be treated as if cast in concrete; we believe strongly that healthy parental involvement activities grow and change over time. However, well-conceived preliminary statements of the intended role for parents in a functional area guide the initial development of activities.

## Specify Parent Roles

There are several aspects of setting up meaningful roles for parents. *To the degree possible, parents, teachers and administrators should be involved right from the beginning in defining parent roles.* Since all three groups have a stake in the effectiveness of parental involvement and will have to cooperate in making it work, they should all be represented in the discussions that lead to the specification of roles.

**Role statements should include examples of specific tasks and responsibilities for parents.** It's not sufficient, for instance, to state that classroom aides will assist teachers in the instruction of students. The statement should also list examples of the range of concrete activities in which classroom aides could become involved. The goal here is to identify, not prescribe, some possible tasks that will inform an eventual plan of action.

**Role statements should be agreed upon by parents, staff and administrators.** A district or school that has involved representatives from all three interest groups in the development of a role will have gone a long way toward satisfying this need. Even so, it helps to provide some means for other members of the three populations to review the proposed statements to be sure that responsibilities are feasible and desirable.

## Communicate Roles to Parents, Staff and Administrators

The best laid plans cannot be carried out unless they are clearly presented. Since it is likely that only selected parents and staff will be involved in developing a role, great care should be taken to communicate role statements to a widespread audience. Coordinators should try to inform not only those individuals who might eventually participate in an activity but also those individuals who could be indirectly affected by parental involvement such as district administrators.

# D. Recruit, Select and Assign Parent Participants

The first three "vital ingredients" constitute the planning or design stage of your parental involvement work. At this point you've got to secure some actual participants. Simply stated, parents can't get involved in programs about which they know nothing. Even when they know about activities, parents often need some special encouragement to participate. And if recruitment goes particularly well, districts or schools may need to develop some strategies for selection and/or assignment because they will have an abundance of interested parents.

### Recruit Parents

*The first step in satisfying this "vital ingredient" is to inform as many parents as possible about the opportunities that exist for them in the parental involvement program.* We are referring here to advertising strategies that will let parents know of the activities that have been designed. Our study showed, though, that simply publicizing opportunities is not enough to guarantee high levels of involvement. Districts and schools need to conduct active, coordinated recruitment efforts to stimulate participation. They must reach out and spark interest among potential participants instead of assuming that parents will come to them.

The most successful districts and schools in our study employed a variety of methods in their recruitment efforts. The *most common method of effective recruitment seems to be extensive personal contact with parents.*

Further, in many successful districts, advertising and recruitment were coordinated by a single person with deep ties into the community, usually the parent coordinator.

## Select Participants

Not every activity requires the participation of all candidate parents (e.g., aides, advisory groups). Once parents have been attracted and identified, selection decisions sometimes have to be made. The nature and extent of these decisions depend of course on such factors as the number of candidates, the type of activity and any requirements for membership or participation. In general, though, *selection procedures should be devised to evaluate the availability, enthusiasm and probable skill levels of parents, in light of a goal of fostering the maximum involvement of interested, qualified parents.* For example, some study schools set up screening committees composed of a principal, teacher and parent leader to select parent aides. We use the phrase "probable skill levels" purposefully; parents can't always be expected to possess all the skills necessary to step into positions of responsibility in the educational process. However, if "training" (the "vital ingredient" to be discussed next) is done carefully, then skills can be developed in energetic parents.

## Assign Participants

In most of the functional areas the last step in securing the actual participation of parents involves assignment. The individual responsible for coordination, in effect, puts on a matchmaker's hat. *Specific parent interests, free time and probable skills are matched to the specific openings in the program.* For example, after parents have been screened for a classroom volunteer program, they will have to be assigned to particular classrooms on the basis of the personal characteristics mentioned above as well as the needs of individual classrooms. No matter how they conducted matchmaking, most of the successful sites let parents and staff know about proposed assignments before implementing them. This courtesy seemed to create a positive impression that coordinators were sensitive to the individual needs and desires of participants.

# E. Train Parents and Staff

One of the study's most clear-cut findings was that effective, well-planned training lies at the heart of successful parental involvement. Nearly every site that had meaningful programs of parental involvement in place had fortified the programs with intensive training efforts. These efforts tended to be frequent and ongoing as opposed to one-shot affairs. They tended to include sessions held before participation in an activity (preservice) and sessions held during participation (inservice). Furthermore, at the most successful sites, training sessions were provided to both parents and staff. These districts and schools recognized that just as not all parents are ready to assume major responsibilities in the educational process, not all staff members know how to work with and utilize parents.

Training sessions can serve a variety of purposes for staff and parent participants. *Training provides general information on overall responsibilities and duties.* The clearer and more detailed the understanding of respective roles on the part of parents and staff, the more efficiently activities proceed. In particular, preservice training on this subject eliminates much of the confusion that is associated with initiating an activity.

*Training provides participants with the specific skills, techniques and strategies that will enhance their ability to perform designated duties.* Frequent inservice training in this area not only conveys important content but also rejuvenates the spirits of participants.

*Parent training can overcome a pervasive concern on the part of many teachers and administrators that dealing with parents who may be inexperienced in school operations is too time consuming.* By providing a basic set of common experiences and skills, a training program assures staff that parents will be prepared to take on significant school-related tasks. Similarly, staff training on how to communicate and work with parents makes parents feel more comfortable about working with staff.

As you design training activities, there are a few things to keep in mind. First, whenever possible, part of the training package for a functional area should include workshops in which participating parents and staff work and problem-solve together. This will contribute to building the close, cooperative working relationships that are critical to the success of parental involvement activities. Second, use the information gathered from first-hand monitoring and evaluation of program activities (to be discussed in Section G) to help plan inservice training. Finally, it is a good idea to structure some time for assessment into your training efforts themselves. In other words, plan on soliciting the opinions and advice of trainees concerning the value of training activities. This feedback will help you in designing training that is fresh and relevant.

## F. Establish Communication Channels

Because effective communication is so important, we devote an entire chapter in this handbook (Chapter 1, Creating Positive Home-School Relationships) to improving general communication between home and school. This "vital ingredient" focuses more narrowly on the communication channels needed to sustain specific parental involvement activities. Such channels are just as important to the health of a parental involvement program as open communication is to the health of home-school relations. Meaningful communication can take place through informal exchanges as well as through officially established channels.

Our work suggests that there are three areas of communication vital to the success of parental involvement.

## Encourage Communication Between the School and Participating Parents

Districts and schools with successful programs of parental involvement make sure that participants don't feel as if they're operating in a vacuum. They are as careful about informing involved parents about district policies and events as informing members of the teaching staff. For example, such districts and schools in our study often included parent leaders on mailing lists for district notices, announcements and policy directives. *Being informed about district operations aids parents in performing designated duties; it also demonstrates to parents that they are valued members of the school community.*

## Encourage Communication Between Participating Staff and Parents

This type of communication centers on the tasks and responsibilities associated with involvement in an activity area. Sometimes this communication is one-way, with parents receiving information from staff that might assist them in carrying out certain tasks. A parent coordinator, for instance, might give a pamphlet on how to run effective meetings to members of the advisory group. More often this communication is two-way, with information-sharing going on between staff and parents. For example, a district might encourage teachers to hold periodic planning meetings with their parent aides. *The initial goal here is to build rapport between staff and parents. Eventually, parent-staff communication can focus on real problem solving with a free exchange of ideas and possible solutions.*

## Encourage Communication Among Participating Parents

Since they are peers, participating parents can comfortably share with one another their problems and concerns. Since they are also frequently working under similar conditions toward similar goals, participating parents can share valuable experiences and successful practices. As an example, one successful district in our study scheduled monthly meetings and provided a meeting place for its parent aides. *Exchanges among participating parents often are an important source for cross-fertilization of ideas.* In addition, parents' morale is boosted by understanding that others are encountering some of the same problems, frustrations and rewards as they.

# G. Support Ongoing Activities

For any group of people working toward a common goal, the supportiveness of the environment is a major factor in determining effectiveness. A group that can count on essential services is more likely to achieve its objectives. So it goes with parents participating in parental involvement activities. We learned that successful parental involvement takes far more than good will on the part of districts and schools. They also need to commit resources for getting parents involved and keeping them involved. We term these resources "support services." More specifically, there seem to be two kinds of important support services.

## Provide Material Support

Recognizing that parents are often busy people whose participation in a functional area forces them to make sacrifices, many successful districts try to make parents' involvement easier by offering a variety of special services. For example, some districts we observed provided babysitting or transportation services to make it more convenient for parents to attend activities. Others made space available in the school for a parent room that parents could use as their own lounge, training center and resource room.

Another form of material support that promotes parental involvement in some activities is recognition. By holding events such as annual awards banquets or getting local press coverage for special activities, successful districts and schools let individual parents know that their efforts in the parental involvement program are appreciated. *By publicizing the benefits that parental involvement produces for students, staff and parents themselves, districts sustain enthusiasm for parental involvement programs.*

## Monitor/Evaluate Activities

The most successful parental involvement programs in our study continually assessed themselves and changed on the basis of those assessments. Parent participants need to know how they're doing and how they might improve; decision makers need to know how a parental activity is doing and how it might be improved.

Providing information for either purpose is not a straightforward matter. It is often easier to let individuals or events assume a momentum of their own, basing present operations on "what has always been done in the past." But ongoing monitoring and evaluation, whether through formal or informal means, is needed if activities are to adapt to changing conditions. *In addition, there is strong evidence to suggest that the more frequent the feedback from monitoring the better; potential problems are not allowed to take root.* Finally, information from monitoring can demonstrate the worth of an activity to administrators and school board members.

The network of support services that you establish will of course depend on your local needs and constraints. But whatever services you come up with, be sure to let people know of their availability. On the one hand, knowing of support services may allow certain parents to participate. On the other hand, this knowledge may indicate to all involved that the district or school is committed to parental involvement.

## Conclusion

You are now acquainted with the handbook's seven key elements. By the time you complete the following chapters, these elements will seem like old friends. This is because the "vital ingredients" are the principal organizers for the rest of the chapters in the book. Each chapter devoted to a form of parental involvement is divided into seven sections, corresponding to a "vital ingredient." These sections describe actual practices that proved to be effective at our sites in satisfying a particular ingredient.

# 3 Involving Parents in School Support

- *Fund-Raising: Parents raise money to help support school activities or to provide materials and equipment. This is also a way to get the greater community involved, such as by having the local business community donate raffle prizes.*
- *Direct Assistance: Parents paint classrooms, distribute clothes to children who need them, repair playground equipment or help out in the office or library.*
- *Child Supervision: Parents accompany children on field trips, on trips to the dentist or in the lunchroom.*
- *Resource Teachers: Parents instruct students or other parents in music, crafts and dance. Parents come to the classroom to talk about their jobs and hobbies.*
- *Political Support: Parents write letters to government or private organizations concerning policies and programs, or they lobby the School Board to support issues.*
- *Social or Cultural Events: Parents sponsor or assist in events such as assemblies, dinners and holiday celebrations. They sew costumes, prepare food, make decorations and organize these activities.*

## What Is School Support?

School support in this handbook means parent volunteer activities that do not involve the academic instruction of children. Parents can volunteer for such support activities as bake sales, letter-writing campaigns, holiday dinners, decorating the school for special events or chaperoning students on field trips. Parents can support an individual classroom, the school as a whole or the entire district. The goal of all these activities is the same: to provide economic, political or moral support for the schools.

This kind of volunteer work is important for several reasons. Since it is the traditional way in which parents have been involved with schools, both parents and staff tend to feel comfortable participating. It serves as a way to reach out to parents—particularly to parents who may not feel comfortable in the school setting or who choose not to get involved in advisory groups or the instruction of children. It provides an opportunity for new parents to participate in the school while they are becoming more familiar with it. Volunteering to help the school may be a parent's first step toward other forms of involvement.

In addition, school-support activities are attractive because they are usually focused and short-term. For example, if parents are asked to help with a holiday dinner, they know that the request is for a designated period of time rather than an ongoing responsibility. School-support activities also are useful for parents who are unable or reluctant to attend school functions. Such parents can work conveniently on some activities at home.

## What Is Successful Parental Involvement in School Support?

*Most parents should be involved in at least one activity that contributes to the economic, political, or moral support of the school.*

We found an immense variety of school-support activities—many different types requiring a wide range of time commitments from parents. But successful activities had these elements in common:

It is important for *most parents* to help in order to obtain and demonstrate broad-based support. In some activities, such as letter-writing campaigns or fund-raising events, this is critical to success. Unless many people participate in some way, it is less likely that your goals will be met. Also, unless most parents participate, responsibility rests on a few shoulders. Care should be taken that too much does not get heaped on a few very active parents. They may burn out and leave a leadership gap that would be hard to fill. Finally, broad-based support gives schools access to many parent resources.

The second part of success in school support is parental *involvement in at least one activity.* Most parents work, so they have limited time to provide services or resources to the schools. But participation in one activity is an attainable minimum goal, since many school-support activities are of short duration and have very specific goals. Therefore, they provide opportunities for parents who are only able to make (or only want to make) a short-term commitment.

*Contributing to the economic, political and moral support of the school* implies that support activities are meaningful to the school's continued functioning. Schools always require moral support—parents willing to express their belief in the school's objectives and goals—and occasionally they require economic and political support. If schools need more resources than their budgets allow, parents can contribute in meaningful ways—repairing playground equipment, chaperoning children on field trips, recruiting other parents to attend a fund-raiser, etc. Political support such as circulating a petition may be critical to the very existence of specially-funded educational programs.

# VITAL INGREDIENTS FOR SUCCESS

## A. Provide Coordination for Activities

Coordination for school-support activities requires that someone plan each activity and see that all the necessary arrangements are made. Coordination also means that each activity is planned in relationship to other activities in the school or district.

First, a coordinator of school support recruits parents, publicizes the activities and irons out the details of where, when and how the activities will take place. For example, if parents have volunteered to bring refreshments to a meeting, someone should make sure that the parents bringing refreshments know how much food to bring, where to bring it and when the meeting is to take place. If parents need child care services or transportation, the coordinator would make these arrangements.

Second, a coordinator considers other school activities in scheduling school support. To avoid overwhelming parents with too many requests for their time and services, any activity is scheduled in accordance with activities sponsored by other school or district groups. Events should not take place too close to those of other organizations because parents may not be able to participate in more than one or two activities within a given time period. For instance, a school may schedule a field trip to a nearby farm for the first Saturday of the month. If the district is also sponsoring a carnival for that day, many parents may decide to attend that event instead of the field trip.

# What Works: Successful Practices

## ■ Teachers, Aides and Volunteers

Classroom teachers and aides coordinate school-support activities taking place in their own classrooms. Teachers send notices home asking parents to come to the class to talk about their careers or to help decorate the room. Teachers or aides ask parents to make things at home for students to use, such as home-sewn costumes or food for a holiday event. Another effective strategy is to have a homeroom mother who organizes other parents for such activities as cooking items for bake sales or painting the classroom.

## ■ Parent Groups

A parent advisory group often is responsible for developing support activities through the entire group or a subcommittee. The group establishes an overall volunteer program and coordinates specific activities. One way to avoid conflict among different activities is to have overlapping memberships in school groups. The parent advisory group can have the president of the PTA as a member. (But be careful about overworking people!) Joint meetings at which support activities are discussed and coordinated are helpful. Written memos and notices can be distributed among all groups. Such practices allow all groups to be aware of each other. Consequently, they do not sponsor activities that duplicate or coincide with those of other groups.

## ■ Parent Coordinators

District parent coordinators schedule and plan some support activities for all schools in the district. They are able to avoid scheduling conflicts and duplication of efforts. Similarly, school-based parent coordinators generally are responsible for organizing specific support activities. They schedule the activity, contact parents for help and get them to participate, and supervise and support the activity as needed. They are responsible for a wide range of activities, from recruiting parents through bringing refreshments to meetings to organizing parent letter-writing campaigns.

## ■ School Staff Members

The principal may coordinate specific support activities particularly if parents are to work in the school. The principal decides on what assignments are most appropriate for volunteers and where they are most needed. Principals typically know what is going on at the school so their participation in coordination is critical. Other staff people, such as resource teachers, nurses or social workers, may coordinate their own activities. A resource teacher can coordinate parents making reading materials for a parent-child learning center. A nurse can coordinate a "Health Fair" in which parent volunteers assist in providing information on health education or available community health services.

## ■ Master Calendar

Maintaining a district or school master calendar of parent-related events assists in coordination. Major yearly events such as a holiday party, and more frequent ones like parent group meetings, are placed on the calendar, and events planned later are scheduled so they will not conflict with what has already been planned.

# B. Assess Needs and Resources

There are two steps in organizing school-support activities that match parent resources to school needs.

First, find out what needs to be done. To get a global picture of what the needs and resources of both groups are, assessment should include both parents and staff. This is important so that activities serve a purpose—either there is a need for the activity or an interest in it.

Second, find out what people can and will do. For instance, if landscaping the school yard is needed, parents who are willing to donate the necessary supplies or who have the free time and enjoy gardening should be recruited. More than likely they will participate. Some parents may have particular talents, such as baking. If the school decides on a bake sale for raising money, those parents should be recruited.

## What Works: Successful Practices

### ■ Assessment Techniques

Informal assessment is accomplished by observation or word-of-mouth. For instance, a teacher knows volunteers are needed for a student program to make costumes, prepare food or design announcements. Through informal contacts the teacher asks parents if they know someone who sews, cooks, draws, etc. Teachers, aides, homeroom mothers and parent groups use informal techniques quite effectively, because they know many parents and have close relationships with individual parents.

Formal assessment has parents and staff members complete surveys to determine needs and interests. Staff members are asked to identify areas where volunteers could help: clerical tasks, supervising students, recruiting other parents or preparing materials for student games. For parents these kinds of questions are asked: "Would you keep the library books shelved?" "Would you chaperone students on a field trip?" "Would you talk to a class about your job?" In a formal assessment, the written record of needs and talents helps determine the scope of volunteer activities and defines who can carry out particular assignments.

### ■ Resource Bank

A resource bank matches needs to sources of assistance. The coordinator of support activities maintains an index card file system. Parents are identified as having particular talents, such as cooking, dancing or translating, and as having specific resources, such as working at a zoo and able to bring animals to school, or owning a hardware store and able to furnish certain supplies. A cross-index system is prepared with persons listed under activities for which they are suited. The activities include (1) social events, (2) supervision of students, (3) fund-raising, (4) clerical and school-improvement services, (5) political action and (6) acting as a resource teacher.

Some activities are spur-of-the-moment and are not planned in detail. With a resource bank, the activity coordinator has a head start in locating parents to contact.

# C. Specify and Communicate Parent Roles

For school-support activities to be most effective, parent roles must be specified and communicated. By establishing clear expectations for parents' duties, you minimize the possibility of confusion, frustration or inefficiency in support activities. Parents will also feel they are making a recognized and valued contribution to the schools. This feeling, in turn, will help to increase the amount of time and effort that parents expend in school-support activities.

## Specify Parent Roles

It is important that parent coordinators, school administrators, teachers and parent volunteers know precisely what volunteers are to do. School personnel then can make the best use of parents' time and can provide support and advice to parent volunteers.

## What Works: Successful Practices

■ Special Support Component
The school or district establishes a special component for school-support activities. A parent coordinator (or a school/district administrator) monitors school-support activities, making sure they run smoothly, and serves as an advocate with the district administration.

■ Job Descriptions
Informal job descriptions are developed by the person responsible for school-support activities. A description lists the skills considered important in that job, the full range of duties and the level of time commitment that will be needed. In composing job descriptions, it is useful to get input from people who will be working with the parent volunteer and people who have performed the job before.

■ Input from Advisory Group
A particularly effective way to get input regarding school support is to ask parent advisory groups to offer suggestions and to react to job descriptions before they are finalized. Advisory groups have a great deal of contact with the parent population and, at the same time, are aware of school needs.

### Communicate Parent Roles

Once you have specified the school-support roles for parents, communicate these roles to potential volunteers. Parents then will know exactly what volunteers will be asked to do, when and where the activities will take place, and how volunteers will be expected to fulfill their roles. This avoids last-minute confusion and delays, improves the quality of effort and makes the best use of parents' time. You are also likely to get more volunteers since people are more willing to volunteer if they know exactly what they are getting into.

## What Works: Successful Practices

■ **Support Pamphlet**
Brief job descriptions for parent volunteers are placed in a pamphlet for distribution to the PTA, civic, religious and other groups that include parents. Pamphlets are sent home with students, perhaps during the first week of school. In addition to job descriptions the pamphlet should cite the benefits of volunteering (both for parents and for the schools) and identify parents who have been active in the past.

■ **Support Handbook**
The school or district provides each volunteer with a handbook for school-support activities. This handbook includes brief rationales and descriptions for all activities, names and phone numbers of persons who are responsible for directing or monitoring the activities, and a blank section for parents' notes.

■ **Advisory Group Meetings**
Since parent advisory groups often include prominent parent leaders, these groups should know what school-support activities are planned. It's a good idea to make a special presentation to these groups describing your assessment for parents' and schools' needs and resources, proposed roles for volunteers and plans for communicating these roles to parents. Advisory groups are very helpful in "getting the word out" to the parent population.

■ **Conferences**
Parent volunteers meet with the people they will be working with—other parents as well as school staff. These meetings enable everyone to understand and agree on what the volunteer will be doing and when. These meetings also enable everyone to see how the volunteer's activities fit into the overall educational program.

# D. Recruit, Select and Assign Parent Volunteers

Recruiting many parents is crucial if school-support activities are going to be successful. Some support activities, such as fund-raising, are not likely to succeed unless most parents are involved. More generally, school-support volunteers and attendees often become the parent pool for other parental involvement activities.

There are various methods for recruiting parents. You will have to select the best methods for your particular community—how to reach the most parents and be effective in gaining their participation. We suggest that you use a variety of recruitment strategies. What works for some parents may not work for others. If more than one method is used, it is likely that more parents will be successfully recruited.

Finally, once parents begin to volunteer you will have to match their skills and interests with activities. If you have carefully assessed parents' and schools' needs, and if parents have responded to specific job descriptions, then the matching tasks will not be too difficult. It's also a good idea to ask parents to specify several activities they are interested in, so that if you have more volunteers than you need for an activity you can ask some of them to work on another activity.

## What Works: Successful Practices

### ■ Personal Contacts

Personal contacts are effective ways to reach parents. People are more likely to respond to face-to-face or phone requests than to written notices. Also, people like to feel special. Approaching someone on an individual basis makes that person feel that his or her particular skills are desired. Such contacts are also effective because they permit parents to ask questions or offer suggestions. That is, parents have a chance to give feedback and get clarification.

Included in this category are both home visits and telephone calls. Home visits are typically made by parent coordinators who recruit parents for support activities along with recruiting them for parent education classes and parent advisory group meetings. Parents, of course, can also act as home visitors, recruiting other parents to participate. Parent coordinators also call individual parents and parents telephone each other as well. A particularly effective practice is a "calling tree," where each parent calls two or three other parents who call two or three others until all parents are contacted.

Often parents learn of support activities spontaneously. The principal stops them in the hall and mentions an activity; teachers make requests for parents' support when they come to pick up their children; a parent spreads the word upon meeting another parent in the supermarket. Word-of-mouth works best as a supplement to more systematic recruitment practices.

### ■ Announcements

Newsletters that are sent to all parents frequently contain announcements of upcoming events, with "advertisements" for volunteers. Local media are also used as a recruitment tool. Notices are placed in the local paper, and coverage of activities is broadcast on a local radio or TV station.

Notices are sent home for specific activities. One effective practice is to have students write invitations to their parents to come to school for social events, meetings, etc.

Announcements are posted in places where parents go, such as a parent room or a house where parents often meet (for classes in parenting, sewing, etc.). To attract other parents, notices are posted in and around the community—the local recreation center or market.

■ **Documents**
Some schools develop handbooks, pamphlets and brochures describing the ways in which parents can help and why they should. These documents are developed by parents and/or staff. They outline the activities, name the person that interested parents should contact and mention any support services that may be available, like child care. They also identify, with pictures, if possible, parents who have been recently recognized or received awards for volunteer efforts.

# E. Train Parents and Staff

For some school-support activities volunteers will need training, either before the activity begins or during their time as volunteers. Training sessions provide general information that will be useful during the activity, such as a summary of relevant school rules and policies. Or the training includes background on an upcoming field trip, such as entrance fees, history of the site, facts about the trip that children may want to know, etc. Sessions can also provide specific information on how to succeed with the activity, such as painting techniques or fund-raising strategies. For some activities, it may be more effective to train a core group of parents, who in turn train other parents. For example, to start a letter-writing campaign, a few parent leaders could be briefed on the intended content of the letters and those parents could then contact others with that information.

Staff people often benefit from training in the use of school-support volunteers. Staff training can cover such topics as how to use volunteers' time most effectively, how to make volunteers feel welcome and valued and how to ensure that volunteers understand what they are being asked to do.

Finally, training sessions serve to reassure volunteers who are uneasy about their ability to perform a task and demonstrate that the school is committed to the volunteer effort. Sessions that include parents as well as school staff are especially valuable for this purpose.

## What Works: Successful Practices

■ **Coordinator Training**
In many cases, staff people who are responsible for coordinating school-support activities are trained to enhance their performance. Coordinators should be knowledgeable in recruitment methods, public relations and

leadership techniques. They also need to know something about the particular activities that parents are involved in, such as fund-raising or painting. Intensive training is especially helpful to coordinators in the early stages of their work as they determine their roles, responsibilities and work styles.

### ■ Parent Training

Parents who serve as leaders may need training in recruitment, public relations, leadership or particular skills. One procedure that is successful is informal advice from parents who have been involved in school support for some time. Guidance from experienced volunteers acquaints new volunteers with the details of their task in a supportive, equal-status atmosphere. Training sessions also provide coordinators with an opportunity to identify those parents who have good leadership skills and who might be interested and successful in other forms of parental involvement.

### ■ Joint Workshops

Periodic group meetings are scheduled. The relevant school staff members also attend (principal, classroom teachers, parent aides), so that volunteers will have a chance to talk directly with staff members and will see that the school considers their work important. The training in these workshops covers the skills necessary for participating in a specific support activity. Feedback is collected on relations with school staff or students, possible revisions in duties, or schedules of parent volunteers.

## F. Establish Communication Channels

Ongoing communication regarding school-support activities is critical. It's not sufficient merely to describe expectations and plans at the outset of an activity. In addition, it's important to maintain regular communication as parents carry out their volunteer tasks—communication between parents and staff, and communication among parents. This enables parents to seek clarification, suggest improvements in activities and share ideas with one another. It also allows staff members to acknowledge the specific contributions of parents. Finally, good communication helps stabilize support activities. When parents realize that their contributions are effective and appreciated, they are more likely to continue as volunteers and to encourage other parents to join in.

## What Works: Successful Practices

### ■ Staff-Volunteer Meetings

When volunteers are involved in an ongoing activity, meetings between volunteers and the staff person who coordinates activities occur on a regular basis—daily, weekly or monthly. The frequency is agreed upon by staff and volunteers. Such meetings help to build a good working relationship between staff and volunteers, and promote a free flow of ideas, problems and possible solutions. They also enable everyone to see how volunteers' activities fit into the overall educational program.

Furthermore, whether the support activity requires only a short time commitment such as a day or weekend, or a longer, ongoing commitment, coordinators should meet informally with volunteers on a daily basis to let the volunteers know their presence is appreciated and to handle any questions or problems.

### ■ Communication Among Volunteers

Volunteers can be encouraged to communicate with each other so that they don't feel isolated in their work. One way to promote communication among volunteers is to schedule regular meetings of all parents who serve as volunteers. These meetings give volunteers a chance to share experiences, ideas and problems with their peers.

### ■ Written Communication

Regardless of how often meetings are held for staff and volunteers, it is also a good idea to send written communications to parents who are serving as school volunteers. Notices, newsletters or brochures announce upcoming meetings, guest speakers, training opportunities, school board meetings, parent-volunteer awards or special school events. Written communication keeps all volunteers informed about school-related events and concerns, even if they haven't regularly attended the volunteer meetings. Such communication also demonstrates to parents that the school values their support.

### ■ Social Interaction

Teachers, coordinators or other school staff members arrange get-togethers of volunteers that are intended for social interaction, not business. Potluck dinners are especially useful at the beginning of a school year as a way to get people acquainted with each other, and at the end of a school year to stengthen volunteers' social bonds, thereby increasing the likelihood that they will remain involved the following year. Less ambitious gatherings are also useful, such as a social hour after school or a meeting during lunch.

# G. Support Ongoing Activities

If school-support activities are to run smoothly and succeed, they need two kinds of support: services and supplies for parent volunteers, and careful monitoring and evaluation.

## Provide Services and Supplies

Many parents wish to participate in school support but are unable to because they live far from the school or have young children. Prospective volunteers may be more likely to come forward, and to remain involved, if they see that volunteers have the necessary supplies and space to work in and that the schools genuinely value volunteer participation.

# What Works: Successful Practices

## ■ Child Care

Schools can reimburse parents who must hire a babysitter when they volunteer. Or the parents can form a cooperative child-care arrangement where one parent takes care of several children whose parents volunteer for an activity. These parents then care for the first parent's child when he or she volunteers for a subsequent activity. Frequently, the coordinator helps organize these child-care arrangements.

## ■ Transportation

In communities where parents do not live close to the school, they must use either their cars or public transportation. Some schools reimburse parents for gas or carfare while others organize carpools.

## ■ Supplies

For the parents to accomplish some support activities, schools offer materials and supplies. For example, to raise money for some playground equipment the parents decide to have a food fair. The schools provide the foodstuffs. The parents then provide the labor—cook the food, make decorations, etc.

Other needed supplies might include paint for fixing up a classroom or paper for sending out announcements. Parents can also seek other ways to get the necessary resources. They ask for donations from local businesses or from other parents. A very important resource is the use of the telephone for personally contacting parents and announcing upcoming activities.

## ■ Services

To recruit parents who are not fluent in English, translating services are necessary. Staff members who are fluent in the second language assist in writing announcements or in personally contacting parents who speak only that language.

Parents may also need clerical and printing services. The announcements and documents need to be typed and a sufficient number of copies printed. If the secretarial staff is willing and available, they can help. If that isn't possible, their typewriters might be used by the parents. The school's copying machine is made available, or a local community business is approached for reduced-price or free copying.

## ■ Space

Parents need the physical space to plan and sponsor activities. This might be provided on an activity-by-activity basis, but a more effective approach is to reserve a space at or near the school for parents, called a "parent room" or "parent house." The typical parent room is used for organizing events, developing recruitment strategies for upcoming events and actually working on a current activity such as sewing curtains for a classroom. In some parent houses child care is provided for parents who are working on an activity. Notices letting parents know about upcoming activities are posted. Parent rooms and houses also offer parents the opportunity to interact with each other and with staff so informal, word-of-mouth recruitment takes place.

■ **Recognition**

People like their efforts to be appreciated. This is particularly the case when parents volunteer their resources and time in providing services to schools. An annual luncheon or banquet honoring the volunteers is one way to show appreciation. A "volunteer of the year" award, or gift such as a handmade quilt for the parent with the most hours, is another way to recognize parent contribution.

Publicity in school or district newsletters is another good practice. Newsletters include photos of parents working on an activity or pictures of the volunteer awards banquet. Local press coverage of a fund-raising event such as a bazaar demonstrates the worth of the activity and is a good recruitment tool for future events.

## Monitor and Evaluate

An excellent source of information on how well an activity is working is the people who work on that activity—staff and parents. By monitoring and evaluating the progress of the activity, coordinators and other school leaders can tell whether an activity needs revision, whether more or fewer volunteers are needed and whether those who are involved in the activity believe it is worthwhile. Information such as this can be used to plan changes in activities for an upcoming year, to publicize successful activities or to demonstrate the worth of an activity for administrators and school board members.

## What Works: Successful Practices

■ **Progress File**

It is a good idea to keep a card file for parent volunteers, recording when they first began their involvement in an activity, any comments they've made regarding the activity, how often they come to meetings or special school events, and what others might have said about that volunteer. Such information enables a coordinator to know when a volunteer's participation is lagging, what the reasons for that might be, which other parents or staff work well with that volunteer, and other facts which are useful in planning and evaluating school-support activities.

■ **Self-Assessment**

At periodic intervals, coordinators take stock of their school-support activities in a systematic way. In interviews, staff, administrators and parent volunteers are asked for their perceptions of success, reasons for success or failure, and satisfaction with their role in an activity. An alternative is to develop brief questionnaires, if you are fairly sure what you want to find out or if there are too many people to be interviewed.

# Examples of Success

In our study, we found a number of sites where these "vital ingredients" were combined to make various school-support activities a success. Here are five examples:

### Putting on a Fund-Raising Event

The parent advisory subcommittee on parent education discovered two major reasons why parents were not attending General Education Development (GED) classes: They had no one to watch their children while they were at class, and they had no way of getting to the classes which were at a junior college at the opposite end of town. The parent advisory committee decided to provide child care and transportation assistance to the parents who needed these services. But there weren't any funds available for this. To get the necessary funds, the parent advisory group decided to put on some fund-raising events. A task force was formed. These parents planned and organized a raffle. They determined when and where to hold the raffle, publicized the event, picked a suitable prize (donated by a local business owner), had some parents decorate the room and make refreshments, sold tickets and, of course, ran the actual event. They were successful in selling enough tickets to reimburse parents for babysitting and carfare expenses.

### Providing Custodial Services

The executive committee of the parent advisory group along with the parent coordinator saw that the kindergarten classroom needed some maintenance work—the walls were dirty, the curtains faded. They recruited and organized a group of volunteers to come in on the weekend and paint the classroom and sew curtains.

### Acting as Resource Teachers

There was a district policy dedicated to preserving individual cultures and introducing different cultures to each other in this multi-ethnic community. The parents welcomed this opportunity for learning about other cultures and offered their services (cooking, dancing, crafts) as instructors for childrens' assemblies, banquets and parent workshops. This was an example of a school need—to carry on the old cultures—coming together with a parent desire—to share their culture with parents and children from other cultures.

### Organizing for Political Action

The School Board wanted to terminate all federal projects in the district. Parents with children in one project wrote letters and attended School

Board meetings to show their support for the project. Now, a parent advisory group arranges for parents to escort Board members to project classrooms to acquaint members with the project.

### Developing a Volunteer Program

Believing that all parents should participate in some way, a parent advisory group developed a volunteer program. Parents helped in the departmental offices providing clerical services, assisted the school librarian, worked with the parent coordinators, supervised children in the cafeteria, playground and halls, and helped the school nurse in sending our health and nutritional materials to parents. In addition, there were activities for parents to do at home if they didn't want or hadn't the time to work at the school, such as preparing refreshments for meetings and making materials for special events.

# Involving Parents in Parent Education

- *Workshops: These are either continuing or one-time training sessions on specific topics. They are held on weekday evenings, on weekends or as part of meetings of parent organizations.*
- *Education Classes: Adult education classes are offered through a local high school, vocational school, community college or university.*
- *Field Trips: Tours are conducted at points of interest in the community, such as City Hall, museums, industries and art shows.*
- *Materials: Books, pamphlets, magazines and newsletters on topics of interest to parents are distributed, or are made available at central locations.*

## What Is Parent Education?

The learning process never stops. Everyone is a learner throughout life, and parents are no exception. Parent education responds to this fact by organizing and making available new learning experiences.

Parent education is made up of activities, workshops or materials that are designed to provide parents with specific skills (sewing, painting, cooking), or with experiences that will help them function better in the home or in the community (parent effectiveness training, community resource guides, health and nutrition workshops). This form of parent instruction is, of course, not new. Schools have traditionally offered "adult education" to parents.

Learning experiences that help a parent function better ultimately help the child. For this reason, parent education provides another opportunity for parents to participate in the education of their children. Parent education programs contribute to parents' personal growth and development. They can meet the special needs of parents new to this country who request information that will help them adjust to a new environment. And they can satisfy parents who have special knowledge and wish to share it by teaching other parents.

## What Is Successful Parental Involvement in Parent Education?

**1. It ensures that a majority of parents participate in at least one activity.** This is another way of saying that the parent education component should be designed so that most parents want to participate. This does not mean that a majority participates in any one activity, but rather the total set of activities is diverse enough to appeal to the interests of most parents.

**2. It is targeted to the needs of parents of children in the school.** A parent education component must focus on real wants and needs of parents. If not, few parents will participate. Matching activities to needs goes beyond responding to just a core group of parents. It means finding out what parents in general want and providing activities that are of popular interest, such as drug abuse seminars and parenting workshops. Or it means designing programs targeted to the specific needs of individual parents, such as English as a second language, general educational courses (GED), jewelry making and foreign languages.

**3. Parents feel that they learn something of value.** The ultimate measure of the success of a parent education component is that parents feel they have learned something useful. Learning can be quite concrete: for example, the acquisition of a new skill such as knitting or dancing. Or learning may be more subjective: for example, a feeling of greater confidence when dealing with public agencies. Either way, it is primarily parents themselves who are able to determine the value of parent education offerings.

# VITAL INGREDIENTS FOR SUCCESS

## A. Provide Coordination for Activities

All of the steps critical to the success of parent education, such as assessing parent needs, finding resources, providing support services or recruiting participants, need strong centralized coordination. For example, an assessment of parent needs may require circulating a questionnaire among parents and then tabulating the results. Finding outside resources may require phone calls to colleges or community agencies to request speakers, set times and discuss details. Many arrangements must be made that parents cannot readily handle themselves. Therefore, before parent education activities can be developed, some form of coodination must be established.

## What Works: Successful Practices

### ■ Personnel
Parent coordinators, principals, teachers, counselors, social workers and home-school liaisons can all coordinate parent education, either individually or in concert with each other. No one way has been established as more successful than another, except that in large schools activities sometimes run more smoothly if they are coordinated by more than one person. For example, resource teachers or counselors handle the structure and content of a parent workshop (assessing parent needs, finding appropriate resources and materials) while a parent coordinator handles the logistics (getting the room, deciding on the date and time and coordinating the recruitment). In smaller schools, a parent coordinator or principal can coordinate the entire effort with a little assistance from teachers or outside agencies who conduct the actual programs. In this instance, however, the person coordinating the entire effort will be more effective if he or she is well known by a majority of the parents, has the time and energy to perform such duties and knows the community well enough to draw on outside resources when the need arises.

### ■ Advisory Group or PTA Involvement
Providing parent education can be a primary responsibility of an advisory group or PTA. Parent education activities are often piggybacked onto regular meetings so that attendance and interest can be maintained. Because these groups are comprised mainly of parents, they are able to make joint decisions about desirable topics and convenient times and places. But, what they generally cannot do is contact and arrange for guest speakers and materials. This is normally handled by a parent coordinator.

# B. Assess Needs and Resources

## Find Out What Parents Need

When planning parent education activities, it is tempting to offer activities because there is someone available to conduct them rather than because parents have expressed a need for them. But successful, well-attended parent education activities respond to the specific wants and needs of the parent population. The school or district must first develop ways of acquiring information. Then decisions are made about programs to offer. Although it is easier to determine the needs of those parents who visit the school regularly, their needs may not be typical. A broad-based needs assessment, whether formal or informal, is important.

## What Works: Successful Practices

### ■ Survey Questionnaires
A good way to identify the needs of parents is to send questionnaires directly to all parents at the beginning of each school year. These questionnaires provide parents the opportunity to respond in two basic areas: (1) what they are interested in learning, and (2) what problems they currently have that the school might help resolve. A checklist of possible problems could be included. The staff considers all responses, matching topics with parent needs and interests.

### ■ Home Visits
Home visits afford the coordinator the opportunity to develop workshops based on face-to-face conversations with parents. Home visits yield information about the needs of parents who don't normally come to the school. They have the added advantage of stimulating the involvement of those who otherwise might be uninvolved.

### ■ Informal Methods
Parents at advisory group meetings can suggest ideas. Workshop or parent room attendees can be polled. Parent aides can also be a good source of information. They often meet with parents, both inside and outside the school, and are in a good position to know the types of training that those parents desire. These are quick and easy ways for the coordinator or advisory group chairperson to gather ideas about the wants and needs of parents.

## Match Parent Needs with Resources

Once parent desires have been identified, the school looks for resources that closely match them. But since, in many instances, the school does not have the capabilities to conduct activities, it should be prepared to find individuals or agencies that can help. Resources can be found within the community (universities, local social or government agencies), within the district or school (skilled parents, staff) or even outside the city (regional resource centers).

As part of the matching process, the coordinator verifies that activities aren't already available elsewhere in the community—for example, in local community centers. If services are available elsewhere, it may be preferable to refer parents to them.

## What Works: Successful Practices

■ **Types of Topics**
There is no limit to parent education topics. Some of the most common are:

**Parenting:** Ways to discipline your child, behavior modification, communication techniques, child development, sex education

**Nutrition:** Choosing and preparing a balanced diet, the benefits of certain foods and vitamins, junk food, maintaining healthy growing bodies

**Community Resources:** What social service and community agencies provide, where to go to find, for example, counseling services, family planning, educational assistance

**Crafts:** Ceramics, needlepoint, woodworking, sewing, leather work

**Language/Speech Development:** How children learn to speak, patterns of language development

**Advocacy:** District and school chain of command, how to get questions answered and problems solved

**School Curriculum:** Reading, mathematics, science, social studies

■ **Types of Resources**
Even with a limited budget, a coordinator can put on training activities. For example:

**Skilled Parents:** Members of the parent group or the community who have the needed skills to train other parents

**Trained Specialists:** University professors, doctors, lawyers, dentists, speech therapists, social workers

**Community Agencies:** Local government, health clinics, church groups, fire and police departments

**School or District Staff:** Academic subjects—also hobbies, outside interests

# C. Specify and Communicate Parent Roles

As we said earlier, the learning process never stops. Parents have a role as lifetime learners. Just as teachers and administrators learn constantly through in-service training and college courses, parents can continue to learn by taking advantage of parent education. In addition to being learners, parents can also be teachers. They can teach other parents dancing, cooking, crafts—anything they know well and are willing to impart to others. In fact, some parents may feel more comfortable learning from other parents, especially those with the same cultural or ethnic background.

## Specify Parent Roles

The parent role as learner or teacher in the school district can be formally stated in a number of ways, as described below.

# What Works: Successful Practices

■ **Policy Statement**
Administrators often make it clear that they recognize and support the parents' role as learner by including plans for parent education in their district statement of policy. These statements typically include a budget for parent education activities, and designate someone to organize and implement them. A district plan can specify the subjects to be offered (discipline, working with the bilingual child) and list resources to be tapped (local college professors, counselors, special teachers).

■ **Task Force**
Parents themselves often recognize their need for information and seek it out. A group of parents get together to decide what they need to know to function better in their community. They then present a request for this information to the school district.

■ **Advisory Groups and PTAs**
Advisory groups and PTAs often include parent education among their activities. They can, for example, include "providing new opportunities for parents to learn" in their bylaws and designate a subcommittee to plan and organize learning sessions.

## Communicate Parent Roles

Whether the role of parent as learner/teacher is stated formally or exists informally, it needs to be communicated to all parents so that they are aware of what opportunities are open to them.

# What Works: Successful Practices

■ **Pamphlet or Parent Handbook**
Information about parent education offerings is included in documents designed for parents. A pamphlet announces the sessions, field trips or workshops that are planned for the year, including date, time and location of each event. When logistics cannot be worked out early in the school year, parents are made aware of planned activities. Specifics are included in later

bulletins or newsletters. The general scope of parent education plans can be included in a handbook.

### ■ Advisory Group or PTA Meetings

Parent meetings are an excellent place to communicate information about parent education. Parent education becomes an agenda item early in the year. A principal or district administrator presents district plans, and parents discuss these in light of their own needs and abilities. Since parent meetings can also be the birthplace of parent education ideas, discussions about them will result in parents being informed.

# D. Recruit and Assign Parent Participants

To be successful, parent education activities must have parent participants. And to get participants recruitment strategies must be designed both to inform parents about the activity and to attract their interest and participation. Recruitment literature may need to be circulated in other languages as well as in English.

Since parents have other responsibilities, notice should be given well in advance of upcoming activities so that they can schedule their time accordingly and perhaps arrange for babysitting or other services.

If recruitment goes well and there is widespread interest in parent education, parents may have to be assigned to particular activities. That's why it's a good idea to ask parents during recruitment to express interest in more than one parent education activity. Try of course to match parents to those activities where they will get the most benefit. If demand for a specific offering is too great to accommodate all interested parents, you may have to try to offer it again.

## What Works: Successful Practices

### ■ Written Materials

To contact a majority of parents, the school should use a variety of written materials—newsletters, informal fliers, bulletins and announcement sheets. Any one of these materials is potentially useful, but when used in conjunction with each other they can be invaluable for attracting the attention and interest of parents. A newsletter sent to the home can include an article on a forthcoming parent education workshop. A follow-up flier can remind parents of the date, time, place and topic of the workshop. In addition, informal notices are posted in strategic locations such as churches, laundromats and supermarkets, and on school bulletin boards.

■ **Home Visits**

Home visits are a very successful way to generate interest on the part of the parents. There are two ways to accomplish this task: (1) a parent coordinator or other staff member makes home visits specifically to inform parents about the planned activity; or (2) such visits are integrated with contacts for other purposes. The coordinator, already in the home distributing tutoring materials or discussing the progress of the student, takes an extra few minutes to tell parents about the upcoming event and encourage their participation. This form of personal contact appeals to parents especially if the visitor is a member of the community and speaks whatever language the parents use.

■ **Telephone Networking**

A creative way of contacting and recruiting parents, without overburdening school staff or parent volunteers, is a telephone networking system. Before each activity, advisory group or PTA members are given a list of names and telephone numbers and asked to call a few parents. Those parents, in turn, are asked to call one more person. And that person then calls another, and so on, creating a large telephone tree.

■ **Verbal Announcements**

An effective way of communicating information to parents about a planned activity is to make verbal announcements at school or at events where parents normally assemble. Examples include open houses, PTA meetings, advisory group sessions and parent room gatherings.

# E. Train Staff

Basically, parent education is training for parents. Therefore, this "vital ingredient" is different for parent education than for other forms of parental involvement. Here it refers to the training of those individuals who conduct parent education.

In many cases, because of their backgrounds, parent educators will not need any special training. For example, a parent coordinator from a neighboring district who is invited to present a workshop on effective parenting will not need training, having already worked extensively with parents. In other cases, some amount of training for parent education leaders may be advisable. For example, a psychologist from a local university, while knowledgeable about the discipline, may never have worked before with parent groups. As a result, the leader would profit from consulting with a parent coordinator before putting on a parent workshop.

Training may also be valuable when parents are used to teach other parents. Many parent leaders have a lot to offer in the parent education realm and are especially sensitive to the needs and concerns of parents. However, they may need assistance in planning how best to present material.

## What Works: Successful Practices

■ Staff Leader Training

The person who arranges for an outside resource person to conduct a parent education session briefs that person before the session. If the parent educator is aware of the age level, interests and concerns of the parents who will attend the session, he or she can gear the presentation accordingly. For example, a policeman who is preparing to discuss after-school safety may stress one aspect of safety for parents of very young children and another aspect for parents of young teenagers.

■ Parent Leader Training

Parents who share their knowledge with other parents may know their subject well, but not have much experience speaking in front of others. They would probably appreciate a quick course on effective presentation of materials. Such a course could cover the use of visual aids or music, sequence of presentation, how to conduct introductions, how and when to ask for questions, how to include a bit of humor and how to tell when to stop.

# F. Establish Communication Channels

Communication is an important element of parent education before, during and after the actual activities. Beforehand, as we have already mentioned, parents and staff discuss parent needs—what parents want to know and learn. During activities, parent educators set up channels for parents to comment on what's being offered and how it's being offered. This may lead a parent educator to revise present plans. Finally, after an activity is completed, communication between staff and participants centers on ways of improving an activity the next time around. In addition, everyone involved may want to discuss the possibility of future follow-up activities.

## What Works: Successful Practices

■ Evaluation Forms

Parents are given an evaluation form to fill out after each parent education session. They are asked to state how useful the session was to them, whether they would like more information on the same subject and what they would like to learn in the future. The responses are anonymous so parents feel free to express themselves completely.

■ Individual Discussions

The person who conducts a parent education session is available to talk to parents privately afterwards. These sessions allow parents to discuss issues they might not have wanted to bring up in the group and to tell the presenter how they felt about the session.

■ **Mailing Lists**

Parents are asked to list their names and addresses on an attendance roster at the beginning of each session. The sheets are then duplicated and sent to all participants so they can contact each other to discuss informally parent education topics or to plan future events.

# G. Support Ongoing Activities

If a parent education program is going to function well, it needs more than just a hearty endorsement. Various support services are needed—incentives or assistance to parents to encourage them to participate, and tangible support for the activities themselves.

## What Works: Successful Practices

■ **Child Care**

Many parents will not attend activities if they have to pay for a babysitter. Schools can solve that problem by arranging for babysitting services on the premises where the activity will be held, or by reimbursing parents for child-care costs incurred during the time they are participating in the activity. Other arrangements can also be developed whereby one or two parents alternately volunteer to sit with the children while other parents attend the workshops. A list is then prepared of all parents who are willing to perform such a task.

■ **Transportation**

If transportation prevents parents from participating in parent education workshops, carpooling or mileage reimbursements can be offered to offset that barrier. Schools help parents form their own carpooling network by generating a list of names and phone numbers so that parents can contact each other. If funds are available, the school can also reimburse parents for roundtrip mileage to and from the workshop, or direct out-of-pocket transportation expenses such as bus fare, by having parents fill out travel reimbursement slips every time they attend a parent education activity.

■ **Tuition and Materials**

One way for parents, especially low-income parents, to continue their basic education is through GED or other adult education programs. The district which sponsors such activities as part of the parent education component can assist parents by paying for the tuition and books that are required for the courses. A district might offer this support in two ways: (1) pay for the courses outright from its parental involvement budget; or (2) contact the local colleges or community agencies that are conducting the courses and negotiate with them to waive or reduce the tuition for parents.

■ **Parent Rooms**
A good way to support parent education activities is to provide a permanent place for them to be conducted. Such a place can be a parent room or a parent house—an area where parents can go that belongs only to them, where they can meet with other parents, keep materials that pertain to their interests and have workshops on topics of their choice. Once an acceptable meeting place has been established for parents, it seems to lead to better attendance at other workshops. Parents come to regard this place as their own and  consequently take interest and pride in whatever goes on there.

■ **Clerical and Printing Assistance**
The district, as well as the school, provides support in the form of secretarial services and duplicating or printing assistance. Most often it is the parent coordinator who requests such services. The district can respond, for example, by using a school print shop for duplicating all of the communication notices and fliers that go out to parents, or by having a district secretary spend some of his or her time typing brochures and announcements for handouts at meetings. Such regular assistance enables the parent coordinator, or other responsible person, to recruit parents efficiently and to provide any necessary information concerning parent education activities.

# Examples of Success

Following are examples of topics, resources and activities that are actually found in our study. They do not exhaust all possibilities, but they do illustrate the types of activities that are possible, even within a limited budget.

## Workshops

1. A community coordinator who had requests from several parents for an exercise class found a skilled parent in the community by word-of-mouth referral. She was hired to conduct two classes per month in physical fitness. The response was high from both men and women because the sessions were held in the evening during the week.

2. Psychologists from a local university were invited by a parent coordinator to conduct a series of training sessions on how to improve communication skills, what to do about an overabundance of television viewing, how to be aware of racism and sexism in school textbooks and how to provide sex education to adolescents. Various instructional techniques were used, including viewing films, reading articles and discussing ideas in small and large groups. This series of four lectures was held in a school auditorium.

3. A school counselor, who had a lot of prior experience conducting workshops, organized her own series of parenting skills sessions. She acquired help from a district consultant, who had similar experience plus access to district materials, and together they conducted lectures on drug

abuse, problem solving, self-concept and juvenile delinquency. The lectures were given in English and later repeated in Spanish so that all parents could take advantage of the information being offered.

4. The advisory group decided to combine a parent education workshop with its regular monthly meetings to boost its attendance. The parent coordinator recruited a paramedic and a fireman to conduct sessions on home safety using films and brochures.

## Field Trips

1. The advisory group sponsored tours for parents, mostly recent immigrants, to local government offices. City council members answered questions and told parents how the government functions, what the various departments include and where to go to find information concerning community-related activities. The tours were funded out of the parental involvement budget and were organized by the parent coordinators.

2. A mothers' group organized field trips to local cultural events and places of interest (museums, state capitol, businesses, industries) to acquaint parents with the community and with each other. The trips were supported in part by general advisory group money (which was acquired through a variety of fund-raising events) and by district funds. These activities did not require lectures from trained specialists, but rather drew upon the resources of the district and its parents.

3. The parent coordinator, who knew the general needs of parents, arranged for district staff to conduct workshops in their own area of expertise. For example, a nurse led a session on nutrition and a teacher lectured on "incidental teaching" using events and objects in the home for reinforcing reading and math skills. Sometimes these workshops were combined with home tutoring sessions.

## Education Courses

1. A federal project responded to the needs of parents by organizing extensive education programs. The parent coordinator contacted community colleges and local high schools to encourage them to waive or reduce tuition fees for low-income parents. Parents were subsequently enrolled by the project in adult studies programs which enabled them to receive college credits or their high school equivalency certificate. In addition, non-credit classes (vocational, business) were arranged through the school district itself, and all fees were waived for project parents. The purposes were: (1) to provide the parents with better skills; and (2) to prepare them to become aides and teachers within the project.

2. Cases existed where federal projects had neither the funds nor the resources to provide their own activities. So parent coordinators and

project directors arranged for parents to link up with district-sponsored, ongoing General Education Development programs, for parents interested in completing high school. The project thus helped parents achieve their educational goals by taking advantage of other programs within the district.

### Materials

1. The district provided a parent training room that included a display of district-related information, but also books and articles on parenting skills, family relationships, nutrition and health, discipline, toilet training, lists of community agencies and the like. The room had cubicles so that parents could work and read individually. Formal parent education classes were also conducted in this room.

2. Some districts received requests to supply parents with a list of adult educational opportunities and facts about health care for children. These districts responded by contacting local community agencies for written materials such as pamphlets and brochures. The districts then sent the information directly to the parents as supplements to the monthly newsletter.

# 5 Involving Parents in Home-Based Instruction

- *Make-It-Take-It Workshops: Parents attend workshops where they make learning games to take home and play with their children.*
- *Idea Lists: Ideas on how to turn household activities into learning experiences are included in bulletins and newsletters for parents.*
- *Resource Centers: Parents visit special rooms at school that contain learning games, books and materials that they can check out to use with their children at home.*
- *Summer Reading Packet: Children take home a packet of reading material at the end of the school year that includes instructions for use and hints for parents on how to encourage summer reading.*
- *Home Tutoring: Parents make game boards that they use at home to help their children master the reading skills presented in class each week.*

## What Is Home-Based Instruction?

Parents are their children's first teachers, helping their children master various developmental skills (e.g., walking, talking) and expanding children's knowledge of the world around them. Parents are the most important people to the child, the people whose opinions and ideas are most valued.

Parents continue to teach their children even after the children go to school and have a regular "teacher." Some of what parents teach their children is different from what teachers teach, some is the same. Since the child takes in ideas and experiences and tries out new skills both at home and in school, the child needs to have all "teachers" working together. Then learning goes forward and the child is not pulled in opposite directions.

Teachers know about learning, and how learners differ in interests and rate of growth. Parents know what kinds of examples and approaches work best with their own children. Together they can form a powerful team, presenting children with a vast array of educational opportunities.

You can encourage teamwork between parents and teachers. By the time children start school, their parents have taught them many skills. In school, however, learning becomes focused on specific skills: word recognition, math concepts, facts about science. You can offer parents ideas on how to reinforce these skills and recommend ways that parents can continue to provide learning experiences that help children toward success in school.

You can approach your home-based instruction program with varying degrees of formality. An informal program might consist, for example, of hints that all parents can use to help their children read at home. Materials sent home would include book lists, ways to use household articles in reading and word games for children and parents to play. A more formal program could require that each parent help children master the math skills presented each week in class. Students would receive weekly assignments for completion at home. Parents would be trained in ways to assist their children and assignments would be returned to school for correction. This section explores some of the techniques that you can use to make parents and teachers effective teaching teams.

## What Is Successful Parental Involvement in Home-Based Instruction?

1. **It involves most parents in at least one activity.** Parental participation in this area is really a continuation of what parents already do with their children at home. The range of activities should be broad enough, and requirements flexible enough, to suit differences in parental interest level and available time. Most parents can benefit from suggestions for helping their children in some area.

2. **It has positive results for the child.** While it may be difficult to link increases in achievement test scores with help that students receive at home, there are other effects of successful home assistance that can be traced. Students whose parents help them at home not only learn more, but also have more positive attitudes toward learning. Attendance is better, students feel more comfortable with classwork and they come to school with greater confidence when parents actively support the learning process at home.

# VITAL INGREDIENTS FOR SUCCESS

## A. Provide Coordination for Activities

A program designed to help parents supplement their children's learning at home requires varying amounts of coordination, depending on how formal it is. For example, more coordination is needed to conduct a home tutoring program that involves exercises to be completed each week and returned to school for correction, than to send home ideas for using math while shopping. A home tutoring program works best if an individual is responsible for organizing parent training, getting materials to and from the home, and coordinating assignments with participating teachers. Whether formal or informal, your program will need someone to organize workshops, recruit parents to attend them, compile lists of activities that can be conducted at home and follow up on specific assignments.

### What Works: Successful Practices

■ Curriculum Specialist
A curriculum specialist is well prepared to coordinate a home-based instruction program. A specialist is aware of what kinds of skills children need to master at each grade level. Also, since the specialist's job involves meeting with teachers to discuss test results and what is being taught, that person is in a good position to know the needs of individual children and of the students as a group. A specialist can devise, or find, exercises, games and resource materials to distribute to teachers for use with parents. The specialist can also conduct training sessions for parents and teachers.

■ Parent Coordinator
Parent coordinators are already responsible for handling the logistics of meetings and other events that involve parents. Since they meet frequently with parents at home and at school, they can recruit for training sessions, transport materials to the home, answer questions and assist parents with home teaching activities. In large districts, parent coodinators and curriculum specialists often work together; the specialist develops the home teaching program while the parent coordinator implements it.

■ School Staff
In districts with no specialists or parent coordinators, principals and teachers assume the responsibility for home teaching activities. The principal schedules meetings, sends out notices to parents and supervises the overall program. Teachers compile materials for home use, conduct training and follow up on specific assignments.

■ Parent Advisory Group
However coordination is to be handled, it is also helpful to have input from an advisory group of parents. The group can be a subcommittee of another parent group, such as the PTA, or formed specifically to help in coordinating home teaching activities. Key responsibilities of advisory groups include suggesting techniques for recruiting parents, serving as leaders in training and helping to monitor activities.

# B. Assess Needs and Resources

In home-based instruction, the emphasis is on meeting the needs of students rather than the needs of parents. The primary purpose of activities conducted at home is to supplement what students are learning at school. An important ingredient of this strategy is to use the results of student assessments to identify areas that need strengthening for each student. For example, you may discover that some students need help with a basic skill and thus attempt to involve parents in reading or math exercises with their children. If you have any bilingual students you may want to emphasize the mastery of English. In the early grades, you may encourage parents to help their children get ready to read. Parents can help their children with specific assignments or participate in a home tutoring project geared toward a particular goal (e.g., the mastery of borrowing in math). However parents participate, their assistance will be more valuable if you assess systematically what children need to know and seek parental help in those areas.

After student needs are assessed, the developers of the home-based instruction program need to determine resources that can be used at home. Many exercises will emanate directly from what is being taught in class (e.g., vocabulary words, spelling drills, arithmetic combinations). Other more general learning materials can be found in homes, libraries, resource centers and teacher centers.

## What Works: Successful Practices

■ Curriculum Guides
Most school districts have curriculum guides. These spell out the skills students are to master at each grade level. You can encourage parents to help their children master these skills by providing exercises to be done at home that supplement what is being taught in class. For example, first grade students, who are just beginning to read, practice word recognition activities at home. Fifth or sixth graders, who are beginning to learn fractions, experiment with recipes that involve dividing amounts of ingredients.

■ **Standardized Tests**

School staff generally administer commercially developed tests at the beginning and end of the school year to assess academic achievement. Test results usually guide the selection of curriculum materials. You can also use them to identify appropriate materials for parents to use at home. For example, if a student is performing "below grade level" in reading comprehension, you can specify appropriate books for the student to read while the parent supervises. If a student is "above grade level" in math, you can suggest extra lessons for the parents to use at home.

■ **Classroom Progress Records**

The classroom teacher or aide, or both, keep track of student progress on a daily or weekly basis. Student records are useful when matching activities conducted at home to a student's current classroom performance in each subject.

■ **Skills Inventory**

The teacher performs an inventory of each student's mastery of particular skills, based largely on test results and progress records, and writes a "prescription" for each child. Some of these prescriptions are for particular activities that parents obtain from a resource center. Others describe exercises that a parent should practice with the child.

■ **Conferences**

Whichever methods are used to assess students' needs, it is usually helpful to set up conferences between teachers and parents. The staff responsible for coordinating home assistance meets regularly with the classroom teacher or resource specialist to outline the special needs of each student. This procedure allows staff to prepare appropriate materials for home use, based on each student's progress through the curriculum.

The school-parent liaison has considerable personal interaction with the teachers, students and parents. The person develops an individualized program for students based on both parents' opinions about children's needs and professional staff recommendations.

# C. Specify and Communicate Parent Roles

The parents' role as teachers of their own children must be specified and communicated to parents and to school staff members. If it is, then everyone will have clear expectations regarding parents' assignments, thus minimizing confusion and inefficiency. Parents will also be able to see more clearly how they are contributing to their child's education and what effects they are having.

## Specify Parent Roles

The parents' role as teacher starts at the birth of a child. Being part of a family is the child's introduction to the world. So, the parent is already established as teacher. But for home-based instruction to work, you need to define carefully how parents as teachers will supplement the work of the school.

There are several means to specify a home-based instruction role. We describe some below.

## What Works: Successful Practices

■ **Policy Statement**
Administrators make it clear that they recognize and are willing to provide for the parent's role as educator at home by including plans for at-home activities in their district statement of policy. These statements often include a budget for home activities and designate staff to organize and implement them. One example is a plan that specifies monthly sessions for parents on helping children to read at home. The plan includes book lists and sources of reading exercises.

■ **Advisory Groups and PTAs**
Advisory groups and PTAs often include the encouragement of home teaching among their goals. The group describes the parents' role as educator at home in its bylaws and designates a subcommittee to organize activities

## Communicate Parent Roles

Although parents continually teach their children at home, they may not think of themselves as teachers. Some parents feel that they are not capable of teaching their own children. Others are unaware of how their home activities fit with what is being taught at school. The role of the parent in home-based instruction needs to be communicated to all parents so that they are aware of what possibilities exist.

## What Works: Successful Practices

■ **Media Announcements**
District policy on home-based instruction is communicated to parents through announcements in newspapers or on radio or TV. For example, a superintendent publishes an open letter to parents in the local newspaper in September stating that parents are important partners of the schools and that schools need their assistance to help the children. The letter describes activities that have been planned and encourages parents to check with their local principal for dates and times of workshops to be held during the year.

■ **Parent Pamphlet**
Brief descriptions of home teaching activities are placed in a pamphlet for distribution to the PTA, civic and religious organizations, and other groups

that include parents. Pamphlets can also be sent home with students. The pamphlet cites the potential benefits of home teaching both for parents and for their children.

■ **Parent Handbook**
A parent handbook provides more detail than a pamphlet. Produced by the district, advisory council, PTA or school, it includes excerpts from district policy or bylaws that describe goals for parent participation at home, describes specific home-teaching activities that parents can get involved in and suggests strategies for solving problems that arise.

■ **Advisory Group or PTA Meetings**
Parent meetings are a good place to describe the role of parents in a home-based instruction program. A discussion of ways to help children at home becomes an agenda item early in the year. A principal, teacher or district administrator presents district plans. Parents discuss their children's needs and contribute to the overall plan.

# D. Recruit Parent Home-Teachers

Since one measure of success for this component is the participation of most parents in at least one activity, you need to advertise widely and use several recruitment techniques. Recruitment strategies may differ slightly depending on the nature of the planned activity. For example, all parents may be invited to attend a workshop on "Using Science at Home," while only the parents of bilingual children would benefit from a session on ways to use English at home.

Some activities require the selection and assignment of parents in addition to recruitment. A remedial home-tutoring program, closely tied to weekly math lessons, may require individual training of parents and follow-up on the completion of assignments done at home. A teacher involved in this kind of program may not be able to give the necessary attention to all parents and students. You may have to decide which students are most needy and select only those parents for participation.

## What Works: Successful Practices

■ **Advertisements**
Promote interest among parents to participate in this component by publicizing it on the local radio and circulating information about it through the use of fliers and notices. A "blurb" in monthly newsletters or bulletins is effective.

■ Advisory Group Meetings

These regularly scheduled meetings are a good place for recruitment activities because parents, community members and school staff are usually present. School staff present the idea of involving parents in education at home. Parent members are encouraged to participate and are asked to recruit other parents by telling them about home teaching activities.

■ Special Events

Cultural or social gatherings are often used to enlist participation. Special events tend to draw large numbers of parents. Examples include orientations, open houses, dinners/luncheons and student dance or drama performances.

If you have a resource center, invite parents on "field trips" to the center. During these visits, staff members explain the activities and materials that are available and encourage parents to take something home to use with their children.

■ Parent Education Workshops

Parent education workshops often include information about helping children learn at home in addition to providing training for parental growth and development. A natural conclusion to a session on nutrition, for example, is the construction of a "food group" chart to help children with their choice of snacks at home.

■ Personal Contacts

Outreach services are provided to any number of parents on a daily basis through the use of parent liaisons. During the course of a telephone conversation, home visit or school conference, staff members encourage parents to participate in home tutoring activities.

# E. Train Parents

Not all parents feel comfortable being involved in day-to-day home instruction especially after their children have started school. Many things get in the way: attitudes that "real" teaching is the school's job and not the parents' job; problems with English; fear that what they teach is not correct or good enough; lack of knowledge about how a child learns and develops; and lack of understanding of the materials a child brings home. In addition, teachers and administrators are sometimes doubtful of parents' abilities to provide reinforcement at home or have had little experience working directly with parents.

Training can help overcome these obstacles by building the confidence of both parents and teachers. Effective training can take many forms depending on the nature of your home-based instruction program. Whether you use workshops or one-to-one assistance, be sure to: (1) demonstrate how to make and use materials; (2) present a broad range of ideas on how to help children; (3) provide resources for trainees to use; and (4) emphasize the importance of communication between parents and teachers.

## What Works: Successful Practices

### ■ Workshops

An informal workshop is developed and presented by a resource teacher on activities and ideas that parents can use to help their children in reading, math and spelling over the summer months. Parents are offered suggestions for teaching their children by using items in the home (e.g., cooking utensils, canned vegetables and newspapers).

Reading teachers hold morning, afternoon and evening sessions for parents of children in grades K-3. Teachers show parents how to make flash cards for spelling words and recognition of pictures.

Teachers and aides specializing in second-language instruction conduct training sessions. Parents are instructed in the pronunciation and meaning of the vocabulary words being used in classroom lessons in the second language.

### ■ Resource Centers

"Resource center," "multipurpose room," "learning place" all describe areas set aside at a central location where educational games and materials are available. Parents check out items after learning how to use them with their children.

For interested parents, a paid aide schedules classes at the center to instruct parents in the use of home teaching materials. Or, parents visit the resource center and present "prescriptions" written by their childrens' teachers to the supervising staff member. The staff member helps each parent locate materials suitable for the child and demonstrates how to use the materials at home.

### ■ Individual Training

Some activities require that parents help their children with a particular skill (e.g., borrowing in math or reading words that end in "ough"). Since not all children need the same practice, home assistance coordinators work with parents individually. For example, parents learn to use a commercial tutoring program which includes detailed instructions for parents with each assignment packet. Or initial training activities take the form of introducing parents to a specific home teaching tool, such as a "game board" designed by district personnel to help parents tutor their children in reading and math.

## F. Establish Communication Channels

Communication is essential for effective home-based instruction. While educating a child is not an easy task, no one has to go it alone. Teachers and administrators have much information. Parents know many techniques for helping their children to learn. The clue here is sharing by setting up a forum for exchanging ideas.

The organizers of home teaching efforts also need feedback from parents. Are the suggestions and ideas they give parents appropriate to their children? Do parents feel comfortable putting them into practice? Are the needs of individual children being met? Home teaching will be more effective if parents, teachers and administrators communicate frequently with each other.

## What Works: Successful Practices

■ **Parent-Teacher Conferences**
Parent-teacher conferences are a time-honored way for parents and teachers to communicate about the progress of a child. This may be the best way to deal with the learning process of individual children. A few rules make conferences most productive: allow enough uninterrupted time to talk; schedule conference times that are convenient for parents; have school work available to illustrate specific strengths and weaknesses; have ready some suggestions for home assistance; encourage listening by both parties.

■ **Parent Rap Sessions**
Parents have many ideas to share about learning activities that have been successful at home. Group discussion sessions can be held monthly, each focusing on a different theme, such as using math skills while cooking or developing reading while shopping. Parents are given lists of possible activities to conduct in each of these areas and then meet at the end of each month to discuss their experiences with the venture.

■ **Social Interaction**
Teachers, parent advisory groups or coordinators arrange social meetings with parents who are involved in home teaching. Potluck dinners are useful for this purpose, especially as a way to introduce people to each other at the beginning of the school year. Less ambitious gatherings are also possible, such as a social hour after school or after PTA meetings attended by parents who are involved in home teaching.

# G. Support Ongoing Activities

As with the other functional areas, home-based instruction will need two kinds of support: material support (services, supplies and recognition), and careful monitoring and evaluation.

## Provide Material Support

Home-based instruction may require less material support than other areas because activities take place primarily in the home. However, it may be necessary to arrange for child care and transportation so that parents can attend workshops. Clerical support may be valuable for reproducing and sending out recruitment literature and teaching materials. And recognition will be important. Parents and students will be more likely to participate in home activities if they know that their efforts are appreciated. They will also be likely to "spread the word," and that may encourage others to participate.

# What Works: Successful Practices

■ **Child Care**
A room is set aside at school where volunteers care for children during workshop hours. Or parents are given a list of volunteers who are willing to care for their children while a workshop session is being held.

■ **Transportation**
Transportation problems are often solved by carpooling. A list of participants is circulated, and parents make their own arrangements. Or else parents are sent a diagram of local bus routes to the school. These diagrams are often available from the local bus company. Another good idea is to have parent coordinators drive parents to school.

■ **Clerical and Printing Assistance**
The district, as well as the school, provides secretarial and duplicating services. Districts often have a print shop located at one of the schools. The print shop teacher produces notices and materials (e.g., reading lists, ideas) to be distributed to parents.

■ **Recognition**
Each monthly district newsletter features an article on ways that parents helped their children that month. One issue shows parents and students sharing learning games in the resource center. Another issue runs photographs of several families at home working together in their "study place."

Luncheons, dinners and assemblies are opportunities to recognize parents who have contributed to their children's learning. A parent appreciation ceremony honors the parents who participated in home assistance during the year. Certificates are provided to parents thanking them for their contributions to their children and to the school. A prominent local person (e.g., politician, superintendent) presents the certificates and emphasizes the importance of parents as partners in education.

## Monitor and Evaluate the Program

Monitoring is especially important for those home activities that are directly related to particular skills being taught in class. It provides information about whether assignments and suggestions for assistance are meeting children's needs and whether parents are having problems conducting the activities. Monitoring can also be useful in evaluating the overall home teaching program. Evaluation will tell you which parts of the program seem to be working best and which "vital ingredients" need to be strengthened. You can also use the results of an evaluation to demonstrate the value of home teaching to parents, teachers, school board members or funding agencies.

## What Works: Successful Practices

■ **Reviews of Completed Assignments**
Staff at a resource center meet parents individually and review completed assignments, and then help choose the next ones. Teachers and coordinators meet and review student home assignments to verify that home assistance is contributing to student progress. Parents using a commercial home-tutoring program mail assignments to the company, which corrects and returns the materials.

■ **Progress File**
Staff members maintain a card file of participants showing what has been completed and what the test results are. At resource centers using "prescriptions" from teachers, staff members call parents when three "prescriptions" have gone unfilled to find out why the parent hasn't followed up on them.

■ **Tests**
Some activities consist of instructional units. Students passing a unit test proceed to the next level. Eventually, the child can test out of the program indicating a year's progress.

■ **Contracts**
Parents participating in home tutoring sign an agreement stating that they will cooperate and complete the activities. The contracts are reviewed periodically by the parent and teacher for adjustments and to determine how the student is progressing.

■ **Home Visits**
The home visit is an especially good way to follow up on the supplemental instruction parents provide to their children. Materials are distributed and collected from parents. Completed worksheets and home-based drills are reviewed and monitored at that time. Any problems or questions that the parent has are resolved.

■ **Evaluation Forms**
Evaluation forms are a formal way to get feedback from parents. At the end of a semester, for example, parents answer a questionnaire on the thoroughness of training and the usefulness of various exercises and helpful hints. They also suggest other areas they would like to pursue with their children.

# Examples of Success

The following are examples of home assistance activities that were being conducted at sites during the study. They are included here to give you some ideas. The possibilities, however, are wide-ranging; be sure to check the Resource Index in this Handbook for more ideas.

### Training Students at Home

1. The reading specialists in one district organized a reading program to be used at home. The activities were to be supervised by parents. First, the child's reading level was assessed by the teacher. Second, the teacher and child selected a book for the child to read at home. The child read the book, returned it to school and made a verbal report to the teacher. Then, the child was given a small prize and another book to read.

2. Another project prepared summer reading packets for children to use to maintain skills learned during the school year. Each child was asked to submit a list of interests. The teacher selected books based on the child's interests and independent reading level. Each parent was invited to come to the school, pick up the packet and discuss the activity with the teachers. However, if parents were unable to come to the school, the packet was sent home with the children.

3. A district presented information to 400 parents about helping their children with reading at home. After the entire group heard an overview, they broke into smaller groups of 10-15 people to receive ideas on what to do. (For example, a parent and child cut out pictures, and the parent then helped the child create a story around the pictures. Or, a parent read part of a book to a child and stopped at the exciting part. Then, the parent encouraged the child to finish the book alone or to read the remainder of the book to the parent.) The small group sessions were followed by another large group discussion where parents obtained answers to their questions from staff or other parents.

4. A school counselor provided assistance in Spanish for parents of first and second graders in helping their children with reading. The goal was for parents to teach concepts in Spanish and then in English. Concepts included colors, shapes and sizes. Parents were instructed to use materials found in the home and coordinate the lesson with normal activities such as dishwashing ("what is the shape of this dish?").

### Assisting Students with Basic Skills

1. The multipurpose parent room was used to help parents provide general assistance to their children. The room contained bulletin boards filled with various instructions and hints for parents to follow when

helping their children improve their basic skills. Bookcases contained free materials (e.g., pamphlets, brochures). The room also included games and activities that parents could use if they brought their children with them.

2. One large "Make-and-Take" workshop was held for all parents by two educational specialists. It included three activities.

—"Shop with Math"—Each parent prepared a shopping list. They added prices to the items on the list from advertisements in the newspaper. The shopping list was to be taken home where parents asked their children to determine amounts for multiple items (e.g., 6 grapefruits at 39¢ each = ?). Then the child was to take the list to the market, shop and pay for the items, including checking change returned. Parents were to monitor the entire exercise.

—"Geography Puzzler"—Parents were given a map of the state to paste on cardboard and cut up into shapes for a puzzle. Parents helped their children put the puzzle together.

—"Shake, Rattle and Add"—First, each parent was given an egg carton and instructed to write a number in each cubicle in the carton. Then, the parent placed two buttons in the carton, closed it and shook it. Wherever the buttons fell indicated the two numbers to be added. The game could be made harder by adding more buttons or making the numbers larger.

3. Staff members at another site met to document which skills each student was working on so they could design activities for the parents. Each activity corresponded to the particular reading level of the child. Various materials were displayed on tables at the workshop. Staff steered parents to the tables that had the materials appropriate for their children's reading level. Then each child was brought to the room. Parent and child engaged in a "trial run" under the supervision of educational staff. At the end of the workshop, parents took the materials home for additional practice.

# Involving Parents in Instruction at School

- *Tutoring Students: Parents tutor students, one at a time or in small groups, in academic subjects such as reading and mathematics.*
- *Leading Class Instruction: Parents lead an entire class in lessons such as alphabet, vocabulary and computation drills, or science and social studies discussions.*
- *Developing Lesson Plans: Parents work with the teacher to plan classroom instruction, such as how to introduce new material and what students to put in which groups.*
- *Preparing Materials: Parents develop such instructional materials as flash cards, posters or practice sheets for use by students and the teacher.*
- *Grading Student Materials: Parents score student tests and quizzes, or grade student papers.*

## What Is Parental Involvement in Instruction at School?

Parents participate directly in the instruction of students by assisting teachers in the classroom either as paid aides or as volunteer aides. In this chapter we use the general term "parent aides" to refer to both paid parent aides and volunteer parent aides. Although paid parent aides receive wages and volunteer parent aides do not, their duties are quite similar: they help students with school work, supervise "drill" activities, grade student assignments and prepare instructional materials. Therefore, we combine our recommendations for parents who assist on a paid and volunteer basis.

Our study showed that parent aides offer important benefits to parents, students and the schools. First, parents can learn a great deal about the educational process, such as teaching styles, strategies for planning a curriculum and ways to assess the pace of a child's learning. Participating in the educational process enables parents to explain future school assignments to their own children—why assignments are important and how to do them. Obviously there is a pay-off for the children too; they are likely to learn more readily and to be more comfortable in school if their parents are actively reinforcing their educational experience.

Second, parent aides provide a very valuable resource to the schools. In most cases, classes are large, teachers are very busy and students need more attention than they get. Parents can be a teacher's "right arm," supervising students, providing individual instruction or helping with homework.

Third, parents can help bridge the gap that often exists between teachers and students who speak other languages or come from different cultural backgrounds. Parents may be able to help explain certain concepts, using an especially effective word, phrase or example. They may also make it easier for other parents of similar backgrounds to make contact with the school and understand the educational process.

"Should my school set up a paid—or a volunteer—aide program?" The answer will depend on the resources available to you. But whether you pay parent aides or not, this chapter will give you some good ideas for improving your aide program.

## What Is Successful Parental Involvement in Instruction at School?

**1. Parent aides are present in most classrooms.** A successful parent-aide program must include more than one or two parents. Since an overall goal is to help as many children as possible and get as many parents participating as possible, you should try to have parents involved in all classrooms. This won't always be possible, of course, but it is an ideal to work toward.

**2. Parent aides instruct students.** Aides may be assigned many duties both inside and outside the classroom. However, to maximize the benefits listed earlier, aides should participate in the actual instruction of students in the classroom.

**3. Aides collaborate regularly with teachers about classroom activities.** Parents bring something special to the classroom: fluency in a language, familiarity with children of different cultures and ability to explain ideas in a particularly effective manner. Therefore, parents can be valuable resources in determining what is taught to whom, in what manner and at what pace. Parent aides need to feel that they are part of the instructional process. Teachers can benefit from discussing their plans with someone who is familiar with the classroom setting. Therefore, parent aides and teachers should collaborate regularly to determine appropriate instructional strategies.

**4. The parent-aide program has continuity.** Although it is possible for many parents to serve as aides for brief periods of time, the quality of involvement is improved with long-term participation. Students, teachers and parents must form stable relationships that continue over a semester or school year. Students and teachers need to know whom they can expect to work with at any given time. Parents need to see the results of their efforts to assist students and teachers. Thus, two or three parents who work at prescribed times in each classroom are preferable to many parents who constantly come and go.

**5. The parent-aide program has impact.** Parent aides should bring about benefits for the school. Students' achievement, attendance and attitude toward school should improve, as should teachers' attitudes. Parents' ability to help their own children should improve and their opinions about the school should become more positive. Some effects may appear quickly, others more gradually. But, in any case, successful parental involvement as instructional aides will have identifiable positive outcomes.

# VITAL INGREDIENTS FOR SUCCESS

## A. Provide Coordination for Activities

If an aide program is to produce benefits, aides' activities must be well coordinated. The presence of parents in classrooms requires careful planning and scheduling. Parents' talents and availability must be matched with teacher's needs. Someone must be responsible for recruiting and assigning parents and for providing services that will make involvement easier and more productive.

Coordination of aides should not be left to individual teachers. They do not have the time or the overall perspective needed for effective coordination.

### What Works: Successful Practices

■ Coordinator

A coordinator is responsible for managing the aide program. This coordinator often operates solely at the district level. However, in a very large district, coordinators should be based at individual schools. Typically, a coordinator for aides is responsible for all activities that are necessary to establish a successful aide program.

■ **Parent Advisory Group**
A parent advisory group helps coordinate the aide program in many districts. The group, or a subcommittee, is responsible for recruitment, scheduling and providing support services. However, school staff retain responsibility for training and monitoring aides and are the final authority on what takes place in the classroom.

■ **School Staff Members**
Another way to ensure coordination is to include this responsibility in the job description of a member of the school or district staff—for example, a principal or overall parent coordinator. Principals are typically responsible for the instructional program within a school, so their participation in coordinating parent aides is critical. A parent coordinator, having deep ties in the parent community, could also assist in coordination, especially in resource assessment and recruitment efforts.

# B. Assess Needs and Resources

To establish an aide program, you will have to get some idea of what instructional assistance teachers need. Are aides needed to tutor students in math? Does a teacher need someone to set up a science demonstration? You also need to know when parents are available to work as aides and what services they are willing and able to provide. Of course, employment as a paid aide requires regular presence in the classroom, but "regular" may not mean "full-time." Teachers may need aides only for certain subjects or certain times of day. Parents who would be valuable in the classroom, either as paid or volunteer aides, may be available for only part of the school day. In short, it is essential to find out what aides are needed and available in your school or district.

Finally, it will be important to match needs and resources, so that aides are neither overworked nor underworked and so that they are placed where they will do the most good.

## What Works: Successful Practices

■ **Assessment Techniques**
Through questionnaires or interviews, classroom teachers are asked where they need help—specific subjects, types of students, times of day or teaching tasks. The results can be tabulated and used to set priorities, prepare job descriptions and support funding requests from school boards, state education agencies and other organizations.

Formal methods are also useful to assess available resources. A good recruitment and selection effort will help you in identifying parent-aide resources. But long before recruitment, you can conduct a formal survey to judge parents' interest in serving as instructional aides and their related experience.

■ **Resource Bank**

A resource bank matches needs to sources of assistance. The coordinator of the parent-aide program keeps a card file that includes past and current assignments for all aides, their specific duties and assessments of their work. Once this system is set up, it is easy to review and revise the selection and assignment of parent aides, as needed.

# C. Specify and Communicate Parent Roles

If parent aides are to be most effective, their roles must be clearly specified and communicated. Of course, the details of a working relationship between an aide and a teacher are best sorted out by those two people, as they talk and adjust to each other. But it is important for a district or school to specify, in advance, what range of duties are to be performed by the aide, and how and when the aide is to do so. This is especially important for new volunteers who have not had much experience in the classroom. They may, for example, be more comfortable if they initially make instructional materials rather than work directly with students. It is also important that role specifications be communicated to both aides and teachers. This will help ensure that the teachers accept other adults in the classroom and that parents feel at ease, knowing what is expected of them.

## Specify Parent-Aide Roles

There are three kinds of instructional duties that can be assigned to aides: (1) working directly with students; (2) helping the teacher decide on appropriate teaching techniques and materials; and (3) working with instructional-support materials. For example, aides may work with students in one part of the classroom or in a reading or math lab. They meet periodically with teachers to discuss progress and plans. Teachers and aides work in parallel, complementing each other's efforts. Another way to use aides is to have them work more closely with the teacher, presenting lessons or showing students how to perform certain tasks. The teacher introduces the major concepts for a lesson, then both the aide and teacher assist students in achieving mastery. This kind of activity requires cooperative planning by teachers and aides. Aides may suggest materials or strategies that seem appropriate for all or some students and may suggest how to divide teaching responsibilities during the lesson.

## What Works: Successful Practices

**■ Job Descriptions**
Each draft of a job description is provided to aides, teachers and other staff members, and their feedback is used in revisions. The finalized job description clearly indicates what the aide's duties will include.

**■ Funding Application Specifications**
If the parent-aide program is to be supported through a specific funding source, such as a federal program, the funding application specifies the duties of parent aides in detail. Preparing a clear foundation for the program in the beginning is an effective way to avoid future confusion between teachers and aides.

**■ Input from Advisory Group**
School or district parent advisory groups suggest duties for parent aides and react to job descriptions before they are finalized. Parent advisory groups will be familiar with resources and interests in the parent population and, at the same time, be aware of school needs.

## Communicate Parent-Aide Roles

Once appropriate instructional roles for parents in the classroom have been carved out, considerable effort should go into communicating these roles. Parents need general information about what aides will be asked to do, and individual teachers and aides will have to agree upon specific classroom duties and schedules.

## What Works: Successful Practices

**■ Parent Pamphlet**
Brief job descriptions for parent aides appear in a pamphlet for distribution to the PTA, civic and religious organizations, and other groups that include parents. The pamphlet includes job descriptions. It also cites the benefits of parent-aide involvement for parents, students and schools, and identifies parents who have been active in the past.

■ **Parent-Aide Handbook**
The school or district provides aides with a handbook describing their duties and includes names and telephone numbers of administrators who are responsible for directing and monitoring their work. (The handbook can also contain blank pages for note taking.)

■ **Teacher-Aide Conferences**
The individual teacher and aide meet to discuss what is expected of the aide. The two of them should agree on the specifics of aide activities. This conference will make the teacher feel more comfortable, knowing that the aide's work will fit in with the classroom routine. The aide, too, will appreciate knowing how his or her specific duties are expected to it in with the classroom routine.

■ **Group Conference**
It is also a good idea to arrange a conference including all aides and the teachers with whom they work. At this meeting, aides get a chance to meet other aides and discuss questions and concerns that they all share. Also, both teachers and aides will see that their efforts are part of a larger, organized program, and therefore will be more likely to accept the goals and requirements of the program.

# D. Recruit, Select and Assign Parent Aides

Recruitment is one of the most important aspects of a parent-aide program, because recruitment efforts determine how many parents will become involved. However, recruitment is not just a matter of publicizing the need for parent aides. To get the most out of available parent resources, your program should offer a variety of opportunities— a range of parent skills and interests, and chances to work just a few hours or many hours per week. Your assessment of needs will of course be very useful for recruitment, since that assessment will tell you what skills, interests and time commitments are needed.

As your recruitment efforts start to pay off, you will also need to develop procedures for selecting parents and assigning them to serve particular roles in particular classrooms. If you decide to include paid aides as well as volunteers in your program, the duties of paid aides should be clearly different so that everyone understands why some positions are paid and others are not.

## Inform Parents of Opportunities

The strategies listed below can be used in addition to other efforts that schools use in recruiting employees. Note, though, that successful recruitment includes a variety of methods, not just one or two. Methods that reach some parents may not reach others. If you use several different methods you stand a better chance of maximizing parent involvement in an activity area. Note also that if many children enter or leave the school during a school year, you may need to mount a recruitment drive more than once a year, perhaps in early fall and again in late winter.

## What Works: Successful Practices

### ■ Formal Policy
The district establishes and publicizes formal policy that encourages parent involvement as aides, so that parents will feel they have a realistic chance for available positions. For paid-aide positions, the district has an "open door" policy that gives anyone, parent or non-parent, a chance at interviewing for the position.

Another successful policy regarding paid aides is to establish a separate parent-aide category alongside the district's regular-aide category. Those in the parent-aide category might initially be assigned duties that require less previous experience than regular-aide duties.

### ■ Job Description
It is very helpful to specify qualifications on job descriptions. The coordinator, advisory group, staff members or others who are involved in preparing job descriptions state specifically what the qualifications are for each aide position, such as:

—is a high school graduate;

—possesses a familiarity with and understanding of the community;

—displays an understanding of the culture and heritage of children at the school;

—in special cases, knows a language other than English.

### ■ Principal and Staff Involvement
An effective way to recruit candidates, especially for paid-aide positions, is to consult principals and other school staff members. These individuals tend to look for likely candidates within the ranks of parents they already know, especially parent volunteers. Thus, two needs are satisfied. One, parent volunteers have a unique opportunity to apply for paid positions; as noted below, this provides an incentive for volunteering. Two, principals and other staff are rewarded because they have identified candidates who they know will do a good job.

### ■ Personal Contacts
Personal contact is always an effective practice. It makes the parent feel that she or he is important and will really add something to the schools. Personal

contact also allows parents to ask questions about the nature of aides' responsibilities. There are several ways to establish personal contact:

—home visits by staff or fellow parents;

—telephone calls;

—informal recruitment by teachers at school or at some other event. Teachers are frequently influential in getting parents to become involved because of their mutual concern over the child.

### ■ Notices to the Home
Mailing pamphlets to the home describing the aide program and explaining how parents can participate is another way to reach parents. Parents can look at the information on their own time. A follow-up phone call or visit is helpful in answering questions and getting agreement to participate.

### ■ Publicity
The need for paid and/or volunteer aides is advertised in school or PTA newsletters, on grocery store bulletin boards, television and radio, and in newspapers and other available media. These ads are bilingual, if necessary.

### ■ Word of Mouth
This "technique" is obviously informal but does provide contact with qualified parents. For example, in classrooms where a bilingual aide is needed, a staff person may spread the word through friends or relations who, in turn, may know of a qualified parent.

## Select and Assign Parents

Once needs and resources have been assessed and parents have been recruited, parents must be assigned to particular classrooms for particular duties. For example, a teacher may want a parent to tutor a few students in reading three mornings a week, from 9-10 a.m. As another example, a parent who only has afternoons free on Tuesday and Thursday must be paired up with a teacher who needs that coverage. Or a teacher who is new to the school may want an experienced aide assigned to his or her classroom.

## What Works: Successful Practices

### ■ Advisory Groups
Advisory groups often perform two important functions in the selection process.

—They help determine the qualifications that will govern the selection of candidates.

—They play a part in the screening process, which influences the final selection of aides.

■ **Screening Committee**
Schools set up a screening committee to interview prospective volunteers
and paid aides. Especially when paid positions are being filled, these
committees should include parents. In our study, we found that parent
members often made important contributions to the work of screening
committees.

■ **Principal Recommendations**
As noted above, a recruitment and selection process that includes principals
usually ensures that the most qualified parent candidates will be considered.
Principals know who has worked capably at their schools in the past and
have a strong sense of students' and teachers' needs. Therefore, principals
can provide valuable input in the assignment process by serving on
screening committees or referring parent candidates.

■ **Rotating Aides**
Both lack of turnover in aide positions and funding cuts can result in few job
openings. Many aides remain on the job after their children graduate.
Although this stability results in an experienced, well-trained aide component,
it excludes many parents with children currently at the school. A solution to
this problem is rotating aides through temporary, part-time positions or onto
waiting lists for paid-aide or appropriate higher-level positions.

# E. Train Parents and Staff

The effectiveness of classroom aides is greatly enhanced by careful
training, not just for the aides themselves but also for teachers. In the
absence of training, teachers often doubt the aides' ability to help in
instruction and planning. And aides, being inexperienced in the classroom, often lack the confidence and ability to work as effectively as they
might. Under these circumstances, teachers and aides place unnecessary
limits on the aides' responsibilities and often grow dissatisfied with the
aide program.

Preservice and inservice training is invaluable. Training for aides
includes information on their overall responsibilities in the classroom,
school rules, specific teaching techniques and classroom management
practices. Training for teachers includes information on how to
determine what activities are appropriate for aides, how to plan an aide's
time while in the classroom, how to monitor an aide's work and how to
communicate effectively with aides. Preservice training is especially
important, since it helps aides to function effectively in the classroom
right from the outset. It also gives aides and teachers a sense of
confidence in their future interaction.

Another advantage of training concerns the parents of students in the
classroom. Parents must feel confident that aides are able to work with
and help their children. Knowing that classroom aides are required to

go through a training program makes parents more comfortable with and supportive of a parent-aide program.

One final note on training: It may be difficult to schedule training sessions at a time when everyone can attend, especially if the sessions are to include teachers as well as aides. Parent aides may prefer evening sessions while teachers may prefer day sessions. You can conduct a formal or informal survey among aides and teachers to see what times and days would be most convenient. Or you can repeat sessions at different times and days so that people can choose when to attend.

## What Works: Successful Practices

### ■ Preservice Training

To prepare an aide for the experiences that lie ahead, a preservice training session is offered at the beginning of the school year. These sessions, normally one to three days in length, should offer the aide something more than content-area training. For example, one preservice session could include information about the school, an explanation of the various duties required of aides and a lecture addressing the sensitivities that aides need to develop when working with students from varying backgrounds. All of these topics offer the aide a sound base from which to approach classroom tasks. A preservice session for teachers covers such items as the effective use of aides in instruction and involving aides in planning. Such sessions can contribute to building positive working relationships between teachers and parent aides.

### ■ Inservice Training

Inservice training, to be truly effective, is offered to aides and teachers about every other month to rejuvenate their skills and attitudes. Workshops can cover such topics as:

—lesson plans and teaching methods;

—making and developing materials;

—teaching in bilingual classes;

—individualizing instruction;

—team teaching;

—child psychology;

—developing interpersonal strategies such as how to offer and accept feedback;

—improving role of performance.

These topics, and others, can be very important in helping parent aides acquire the knowledge and skills they will need to work successfully with students, participate in classroom planning and contribute to teaching strategies. Some inservice sessions should be held for the teachers and aides together. Joint training is beneficial because it permits teachers and aides to continue building the working relationships that are so important in a classroom situation.

■ **Workshops**
School-wide or district-wide workshops are held during the school year for all personnel, to cover such topics as improving human relations skills, developing role performance in the classroom, identifying learning problems, child psychology and even the use of audio-visual or duplicating equipment. Parent aides should be invited to these workshops and workshops should be scheduled at convenient times.

■ **Career Development**
A career development program that is linked with a local college encourages parents to obtain teaching credentials or other certification while helping out as aides. Parents take courses related to their work as aides, while the college gives them credit for on-the-job experience. Such a program is an important way not only of supporting the training of aides, but of offering them a chance for personal growth and satisfaction.

# F. Establish Communication Channels

Effective parent aides need continual, up-to-date information about the district, classroom activities, student needs and the work of other aides. Communication channels must be developed between the district, school and aides, between teachers and aides, and among the aides themselves.

Communication between the district/school and aides keeps aides informed about district policies and events, opportunities for inservice training and possible openings for other jobs. Such communication supports parents in their work as aides and also demonstrates to aides that they are valued members of the school community.

You might think that communication between teachers and aides is automatic, because they are in the classroom together on a regular basis. But this is not necessarily the case, since teachers and aides will both be very busy interacting with students. Aides often perform much of their work independently. Thus, it is important that communication between teachers and aides be actively promoted so that both will know precisely what the aides' duties and problems are. Such communication also develops closer rapport.

Finally, communication among the aides themselves is important. Since they are peers, they can readily share their problems and concerns. They can also discuss valuable experiences and possible solutions to the problems they encounter. But again, as with communication between teachers and aides, communication among aides will be more frequent and more productive if it is actively promoted.

# What Works: Successful Practices

## ■ Written Communication

Notices, newsletters and directives are sent to teachers and aides. They cover a broad range of information from items that are specific to the school (e.g., staff meetings, inservice training, guest speakers) to items that are specific to the district (e.g., yearly calendar of events, employee salaries, new appointments). This communication keeps parent aides and teachers informed about pertinent district and school operations. It also helps aides to realize that they are an important part of the school community.

## ■ Written Schedule

Large programs require a calendar that indicates who is in which classrooms and when. The calendar can be posted in a central location or be circulated to participating parents and teachers.

Also, individual aides and teachers meet to determine the aide's schedule. This method is appropriate for small programs. Although it is less formal than a calendar, both parents and teachers should keep a written record of all schedules.

## ■ Teacher-Aide Meetings

The teacher and the aide communicate well through structured daily, weekly or bi-weekly meetings. (The frequency should be jointly agreed upon by the participants.) Such meetings serve several purposes. They build good working relationships between teachers and aides, they promote the free flow of ideas and they enhance the overall effectiveness of the aide in the classroom. Not only do teachers and aides plan their instructional strategies at these sessions, but they exchange invaluable information about such things as individual student progress, teaching concepts and current developments in the classroom.

Ongoing, daily informal communication is another way of meeting the informational needs of teachers and parent aides. These sessions are not as lengthy as the structured meetings, but they can provide enough time to discuss general instructional strategies for the following day.

## ■ Attendance at Staff Meetings

Aides will feel more a part of the school staff if they are invited to attend faculty meetings. A policy of inviting aides to faculty meetings gives aides the opportunity to contribute to discussions concerning school activities and allows them to learn, firsthand, about issues and policies that affect the school or district as a whole.

## ■ Communication Among Aides

Aides can become stagnant if they are isolated from their peers. By establishing regularly scheduled meetings for aides within the district, you can encourage the sharing of ideas and experiences with peers. Information aides gain from each other may then be passed on to the teachers with whom they work.

Another successful practice is to arrange for parent aides to observe the work of other parent aides, so they can see different materials and practices in action. This serves as a valuable form of inservice training as well.

■ Social Interaction

Meetings of aides and other school staff meet social needs as well as work needs. Potluck dinners are useful, especially at the beginning of a school year, to get people acquainted, and at the end of a year to strengthen social bonds and increase the likelihood that aides will remain involved next year. Shorter get-togethers are also a good idea during the school year, such as a social hour after school or a conversation during lunch.

# G. Support Ongoing Activites

If a parent-aide program is to succeed, it will need more than good will from districts and schools. It will need two kinds of support services: material support, and constructive monitoring and evaluation.

## Provide Material Support

The parent-aide program will be more likely to run smoothly and effectively if aides have the necessary supplies and see that the school genuinely values their work. This kind of support may be more appropriate for volunteer aides, since their participation requires them to make sacrifices without any paid compensation. But even for paid aides, material support is an important factor in recruiting parents to work in the schools and enabling them to do their best.

## What Works: Successful Practices

■ Transportation

Helping with transportation is a much needed service. Schools assist parents in forming carpools or developing a list of names, addresses and telephone numbers that will allow parents to contact one another on their own. Another practice is to reimburse parents for any out-of-pocket transportation expenses (such as gas money or bus fare). Parents can also be encouraged to ride with their children on the school bus, if there is enough space.

■ Babysitting

Schools arrange for babysitters or assist in making child-care arrangements. This may take the form of actually reimbursing parents for any child-care costs, or developing a cooperative child-care program where one parent sits with the children while other parents are working in the classroom. This could take place either at the parents' homes or in space donated by the school.

■ **Recognition**

Award luncheons, teas and other types of ceremonies show appreciation for aides and for teachers who work well with aides. One example is an annual award given to the school with the "best" volunteer-aide program. The criteria for success are that the program has a coordinator, a training program and a ratio of two hours of volunteer service for each child in the school.

Publicity in the local media is an effective way to recognize parents' contributions. Newspaper articles, television programs or radio interviews provide public recognition for aides' work. A particularly effective practice is to have pictures of aides printed in a district-wide newsletter.

## Monitor and Evaluate the Program

By carefully monitoring the parent-aide program, coordinators and other school leaders can demonstrate the importance of the program and tell whether assignments for aides need to be revised, whether more (or fewer) aides are needed and whether those aides and teachers already in the program think it is worthwhile. This information is used to make changes in the program, to publicize the program in future recruitment efforts and to demonstrate the worth of the program to administrators, school board members and funding agencies. For some aides, especially volunteers, evaluation may be handled informally. But, in any case, some form of evaluation is essential.

## What Works: Successful Practices

■ **Progress File**

A card file is kept for each paid aide and volunteer recording when they first started work at the school; the classroom they are assigned to; what their schedule is; how often they attend staff meetings and other school events; and whether they have used certain support services (such as child care or transportation). The card file enables coordinators to know whether a possible change in the aide's duties or schedule is feasible, how well the aide seems to like the work and other facts that are helpful in planning and evaluating the overall program.

■ **Principal Visits**

Because principals are located permanently at the schools and are responsible for the educational program, it is often easier for them to observe teachers and aides than it would be for someone from the district office. Principals personally observe and converse with teachers and aides, provide them with direct, constructive feedback and solicit any relevant input from others. Criteria may already be established and listed on an evaluation sheet. These criteria might encompass overall ability, relationship with children, and attitudes and appearance. The results of monitoring can help determine the areas in which teachers and aides need more training. Personal feedback from principals also lets aides know their work is significant.

■ **Teacher Monitoring**

Classroom teachers have the most constant contact with aides and know the most about their skills and performance. They can use the same methods as those followed by the principals, or they can develop slightly different ways. It is common for teachers to give a list of duties to an aide, then sit down a month later and together evaluate how well the aide has performed those duties. Such a method has proved effective in keeping aides on target and helping them to become more proficient in the classroom. Again, immediate feedback is provided so that aides can quickly change their approaches to coincide with the suggestions of the reviewer.

■ **Advisory Group Evaluation**

A subcommittee of a parent advisory group performs evaluations by visiting each classroom that is using parent aides. Such evaluations are very beneficial to the parent aide because the subcommittees are made up of parents who are likely to be sympathetic to the role the aide is trying to play. Further, because their own children may be in some of those classrooms, observers may be more concerned about the skills and performance of the aide than observers who have no children in the school.

■ **Aide Evaluation**

The coordinator of a parent-aide program interviews the aides themselves to determine in what tasks they believe they have been most successful, in what tasks they need more training, what kinds of material support are needed and other matters. This practice should be combined with others in evaluating paid aides. If resources for evaluation are thin, this practice is a relatively quick but valuable way to evaluate a volunteer-aide effort.

■ **Self-Assessment**

At periodic intervals, coordinators take stock of the program in a systematic way. In interviews, teachers, administrators and aides are asked for their perceptions of success, reasons for success or failure in specific duties and satisfaction with the work of aides. A less time-consuming alternative is to review written reports of the practices above: principals' visits, teacher monitoring and advisory group evaluation. General problems, solutions and other perceptions can be gleaned from these records without necessarily "taking stock" in special interviews. Still another method is to develop brief questionnaires if you are fairly sure what you want to find out.

# Examples of Success

Many of the sites in our study set up effective programs that involved parents in instruction at school. Below we share four examples.

### Providing Bilingual Parent Aides

A school district served many newly arrived immigrant families. The schools held bilingual reading classes for children who were just learning English. Each class was conducted by a reading teacher and a bilingual aide who had been recruited from the parent population. Typically, the teacher presented lessons to the group in English. The aide then explained the concepts and demonstrated the tasks to be done in the students' own language. As seatwork progressed, the aide worked individually with students who needed assistance, using both English and the students' language to clarify the assignment. Periodically, the teacher and the aide evaluated each student's progress with English and designed exercises to be used individually by the students in class or at home.

### Providing Parent Aides in the Math Lab

As part of a remedial program, a school maintained a math lab where students received individual instruction on a pull-out basis from parent math aides. Each child brought a card from his regular teacher listing the skills to be mastered that week. The aides assisted the students using materials in the math lab appropriate to the skills the student was learning. The students also took the skill cards home to practice them with their parents on a specially designed game board. At the end of each week the math aides discussed student progress with the teachers and together they determined which skills each student should work on the following week.

### Providing Aides for Field Trip Instruction

Teachers said they needed help in supervising field trips, so the principal recruited parents to serve as field trip aides. Each aide received a handbook describing the school's philosophy and regulations, procedures for checking in and suggestions for encouraging good behavior. To make aides feel a part of the instructional process, the handbook also described ideas for learning exercises that aides could lead on the ride to and from the field trip site. The principal also encouraged school staff to learn aides' names and placed their pictures on a bulletin board near the staff lounge.

### Establishing a Rotating Aide Program

A school had a surplus of parent volunteers for classroom aide positions, so a part-time, rotating aide program was established. Parents participated in the program for a specified amount of time, usually eight to twelve weeks, helping children go over concepts and lessons introduced by the teacher. At the end of the specified time, each parent aide was replaced by another. The rotating feature of the parent-aide program created a constantly growing group of parents who were capable of working both in the classroom and at home, as teachers of their own children.

# Involving Parents in Advisory Groups

**7**

- *Curriculum Advice: Each year a parent advisory group reviews curriculum materials and plans. The group indicates its preferences, and reasons for them, to administrators.*
- *Budget Advice: A parent advisory group assists administrators in deciding on budget allocations and in choosing among programs to continue, reduce or expand.*
- *Personnel Advice: A parent advisory group participates in interviewing, screening and recommending candidates for paraprofessional positions.*
- *Advice on Parent Activities:* A parent advisory group offers suggestions to administrators or parent coordinators about parental involvement—types of activities, how to attain success with them and how to monitor them.

## What Is a Parent Advisory Group?

A parent advisory group provides advice to or consults with district staff when decisions are being made about district or school operations. The group might include district and school staff members and community representatives as well as parents. Many parent advisory groups get involved in a wide range of activities beyond advising and consulting. For example, such groups are frequently the principal mechanisms for coordinating school-support and parent education programs. However, in this chapter, we only discuss advisory groups that assist administrators and staff in making decisions or establishing policies that affect school services, activities or budgets.

While district and school administrators have the major responsibility for making decisions about school-related matters, many parent advisory groups contribute valuable assistance and support to decision makers. The nature and extent of advisory group participation in decision making depends on a district's practices, policies and procedures. However, administrators who carve out meaningful advisory roles for parent groups received many benefits for their efforts. For example, advisory group advice has helped several districts improve their curriculum materials and instructional methods. Other districts have been able to make critical decisions related to the expenditure of funds and count on the active support of parents because they consulted the advisory group during the decision-making process.

Service on active advisory groups also contributes to parents' personal growth and development. Parent participants are able, for example, to interact more confidently with professional staff because of experiences on an advisory group. Such parents understand better how school-related decisions are made and the constraints under which decision makers operate.

## What Is Successful Parent Advisory Group Involvement?

1. **The parent advisory group gets involved in significant school-related areas.** A parent advisory group ought to participate in making important decisions. Our study showed that the most active groups helped make decisions about: (1) curriculum, or what instructional services are offered to students; (2) the budget, or how funds are allocated; (3) personnel, or who provides educational services to students; and (4) parent activities, or how parents are to participate in schools.

2. **This involvement occurs regularly.** The parent advisory group contributes regularly to decisions on educational matters. For example, a one-time screening of paid-aide applications is not considered successful involvement. A group should be meeting periodically to discuss issues and to make recommendations to decision makers.

3. **This involvement has impact.** Parent advisory group recommendations are listened to and, on occasion, lead to action. In other words, there should be some evidence that the group's advice has actually influenced decisions made by district or school staff.

# VITAL INGREDIENTS FOR SUCCESS

## A. Provide Coordination for Activities

Any group needs a good deal of coordination to run efficiently and accomplish its goals. Many districts make the mistake of assuming that a district administrator or advisory group chairperson will handle coordination. Administrators are often too busy with their regular responsibilities to deal effectively with the logistical and clerical details of running an advisory group. Chairpersons frequently do not recognize coordination as part of their role. Therefore, it is essential that someone like a parent coordinator, the advisory group chairperson or a teacher (with close ties to the parent community) be given direct authority and responsibility to perform critical duties, such as recruiting parents and arranging for training.

### What Works: Successful Practices

■ Selection Criteria
A set of selection criteria helps a district choose its advisory group coordinator. Qualifications include: (1) prior experience with schools or other education-related organizations, (2) membership in parent advisory groups, and (3) ability to communicate well and work with parents and staff. In addition, bilingual projects require proficiency in the target language.
  Procedures for selecting the coordinator vary. Appointment by the district administration is one alternative. Another is to have the previous year's group vote for its choice as coordinator.

■ Coordinator Training
In many cases, districts need to offer instruction to coordinators to enhance their performance. The coordinator should be knowledgeable about: advisory group operations; the role/responsibilities of a coordinator; state and district policies; and parental involvement strategies. Training in any or all of these areas gives the coordinator the direction needed to maintain a smooth-running parent advisory group. Intensive, preservice training may also serve to eliminate a lot of early confusion for the coordinator in terms of figuring out just what his or her role should be and how it should be carried out.

## B. Assess Needs and Resources

The areas in which advisory group advice is needed will vary from district to district. In some districts, decision-making practices and procedures actually prohibit advisory group participation in one or more decision areas. Therefore, it is essential that you conduct a needs assessment to determine the decision areas in which advisory group involvement is both feasible and potentially valuable. This assessment will assist in determining a role for the group (the next ingredient).

Second, you need to take stock of parents' skills and experiences that might help them contribute to decision-making activities. For example, some potential members may have served on personnel committees for other organizations. This kind of information will help you decide how ambitious the decision-making role of the advisory group can be.

Many districts tend to exclude advisory group participation in certain decision areas because they assume that parents are not sophisticated enough. A resource assessment in most of these cases will prove the assumption is false; in other instances, an assessment of members' expertise will identify relevant skills that can be enhanced with a solid training program. A resource assessment can also assist the advisory group coordinator in setting up productive subcommittees.

## What Works: Successful Practices

### ■ Formal Survey Techniques
Through questionnaires or formal interviews, district- and school-level administrators are asked about the decision areas where an advisory group can and should participate. They are also asked why they think such participation would be beneficial. The results can be used to formulate an advisory group role in specific decision areas.

Similarly, potential parent members are interviewed or sent questionnaires that inquire about their skills and past experiences in such areas as curriculum, budget, personnel and parent activities.

### ■ Informal Techniques
Informal discussions and observations provide information that helps you decide in what kinds of decisions an advisory group can assist. Your informal contacts with administrators and parents, your firsthand knowledge of district practices and your experiences in the past with advisory groups all provide valuable information for an informal resource assessment.

### ■ Advisory Group Member Biographies
Short, capsule summaries of members' backgrounds and experiences are developed by the advisory group coordinator. These "biographies" describe, in effect, the resources available to the advisory group. They are particularly helpful when specifying a role for the advisory group, deciding on areas for training and setting up an effective subcommittee structure.

# C. Specify and Communicate Advisory Group Roles

If an advisory group is going to contribute to decisions on district operations, then there needs to be a common understanding about the nature of the group's responsibilities. In other words, the group's role should be well defined and explicit so that parents and administrators alike know what to expect.

Districts that take time to specify a role for their advisory group and communicate this role to all involved reap significant benefits. In particular, the tension and strain between administrators and parents that often accompany advisory group, decision-making activity in other districts are significantly reduced.

## Specify Advisory Group Roles

In specifying a role for the advisory group, it is important that parents, teachers and administrators be involved in defining the role. These three groups need to agree on what the advisory group will be doing. Otherwise, there is a risk that adversarial relationships will form with, for example, administrators feeling threatened by the involvement of the advisory group or parents feeling they should have more influence over decisions.

Once agreement has been reached, a fairly detailed written statement of the advisory group's role in district operations should be established. Such a statement makes the group's responsibilities clear to all involved and serves as a preliminary blueprint for action. In effect, the statement is a job description for the advisory group.

The statement starts out by identifying the broad decision areas in which the advisory group will advise, such as budget or curriculum. Then the statement goes on to describe some of the specific activities that the group will conduct in each area of involvement. For example, if the group is to contribute to decisions about curriculum, it will have to establish a process for reviewing and commenting upon textbooks.

Finally, the written statement should define how much responsibility the advisory group will have in any decision area. Advisory activity can take many forms, ranging from making recommendations to actually making a binding decision. As we have emphasized throughout this chapter, the degree of advisory group responsibility varies according to local circumstances. However, whatever the group's decision prerogatives, they should be carefully described in the written statement.

# What Works: Successful Practices

### ■ Bylaws
The approach used most frequently to establish written guidelines for advisory groups is bylaws. The key is to develop bylaws that describe clearly the areas of responsibility and related activities of advisory groups. Bylaws also need to cite any legal requirements or procedures that affect decision making within a district.

### ■ Policy Statement
A district shows its support and recognition of an advisory group's role by including the key elements of that role in a statement of policy. District policy statements describe the areas in which the advisory group will be working and its level of responsibility in these areas, as well as making a budget allocation and designating someone as coordinator.

### ■ Task Force
Whether bylaws or a policy statement are the end product, a task force is a good mechanism for deliberating about a role for an advisory group. The task force is comprised of parents, teachers and administrators. It permits the cooperative development of bylaws or policy statements. It ensures that all interested parties are represented in the process that leads to formulation and approval of role statements for the advisory group.

## Communicate Advisory Group Roles

Once the role of the advisory group has been determined, agreed upon and documented, it should be publicized on as widespread a basis as possible. This means informing parents, teachers and administrators at large about advisory group responsibilities. In addition, it is worthwhile to let people know of the process that was used to specify the role, so that each segment of the school/community will know that its interests were not overlooked.

# What Works: Successful Practices

### ■ Pamphlet or Parent Handbook
Descriptions of the intended role for the advisory group are included in documents designed for parents. These documents are distributed widely, so that most parents, not just those who will become group members, are informed about the kinds of activities that the advisory group will be conducting. Effective role descriptions for parent pamphlets and handbooks require the translation of bylaws or policy statements into simpler language.

### ■ School Board Meetings
School boards are the major policy-making bodies in districts; their public meetings are often well attended. These meetings present a valuable opportunity for sharing key aspects of the advisory group's role, including

potential decision areas and specific activities. One of the members of the task force delivers a presentation on what the advisory group will be doing. He or she then answers questions and passes out pamphlets or fliers about the group.

# D. Recruit and Select Parent Members

Advisory groups can include teachers, school or district administrators and representatives from local community groups in their membership. However, the effectiveness of advisory groups is increased by having as broad-based a parent membership as possible. In particular, it is important for the group to be viewed by district administrators as representative of all parents who have children currently in the schools. For example, if the district has children from several cultural/ethnic backgrounds, the advisory group should have representation from each ethnic group so that it is considered a "voice" for all parents. Therefore, a recruitment process that affords as many parents as possible the opportunity either to become members or to select representatives is critical.

The recruitment process requires that several people expend considerable time and energy. First, recruiters will have to reach out and attract the interest of parents in general. Then, if recruitment efforts start to pay off, methods for selecting those parents best-suited to serve on the committee will have to be instituted.

## Inform Parents of Opportunities

Recruiters must develop and use a variety of ways to spark the interest of parents in serving on an advisory group. Methods that reach some portions of the parent population may not reach others. If you use several different methods of informing parents, you stand a better chance of maximizing parental involvement within the group.

## What Works: Successful Practices

### ■ Personal Contacts
Members of the advisory group and selected district/school staff talk to individual parents about advisory group opportunities. Telephone calls are one means for reaching out to parents on a personal basis. However, the face-to-face contact involved in home visits is even more effective. Either way, parents appreciate the attention and the chance to ask specific questions about the activities of the advisory group and the time involved in being a member.

**■ Special Events**
Cultural or social gatherings are good places to stage recruitment efforts because they attract large numbers of parents. For example, during the intermission of an evening student music performance, the advisory group coordinator can make a short presentation about advisory group service. The coordinator can call parents' attention to an information booth that will be set up in the lobby after the performance.

**■ Notices Sent Home**
Bulletins or newsletters are useful in reaching large numbers of parents at one time. Frequently such notices are used to spark general interest and are followed up with a phone call or visit at a later time. Or, alternatively, the notices include a phone number that parents can call to get further information about the advisory group. Notices are sent home with the child or, if funds are available, mailed.

**■ Media**
Recruiters put ads in local newspapers, or on radio/television, informing parents of the personal and institutional benefits that come from participation in the advisory group. This is an especially effective technique to communicate with those parents who do not usually attend school functions.

## Select Parents

If you have been able to stimulate widespread interest among parents, you may be in the enviable position of having more candidates than advisory group slots. In this case, you will have to screen the candidates and then select among them.

Factors that can be used in the screening process include: amount of available time; interest in serving, especially as indicated by having been previously involved in similar activities; skills and experience levels (or willingness to be trained); and commitment to the advisory group's role within the district.

Once candidates have passed an initial screening, there must be a systematic process in place to select among them. The best selection process for a specific district depends on community characteristics, the number of qualified candidates and any rules for advisory group membership. In our study, for example, we saw some districts where open elections for group members were held and other districts where the chairperson appointed parent members to the advisory group.

## What Works: Successful Practices

**■ Standards Contained in Bylaws**
Steps to follow in the screening and selection of advisory group members are outlined in the bylaws. By making standards both formal and public,

districts minimize the possibility of misunderstandings on the part of administrators, teachers and especially parent candidates. This is an especially effective strategy if the bylaws are agreed upon by all interested parties.

■ **Screening Subcommittee**
Present members of the advisory group are given the principal responsibility for screening future members. A subcommittee is formed; the majority of its members are parents. The subcommittee assesses the extent to which candidates meet certain standards. After interviewing candidates, the subcommittee identifies those parents whose candidacy it supports.

This strategy utilizes the knowledge and insights of "veteran" parents, while guaranteeing a peer review for parent candidates.

■ **Personal Recommendations**
The chairperson and other advisory group members are asked to recommend parents whom they think are particularly well qualified for membership. District or school staff might also provide reliable suggestions. This practice is often successful because some parents earn a well-deserved reputation for being dependable and interested in shaping policies that affect their children's education.

■ **School-Level Representation**
In some districts service on school-level advisory groups is treated as a prerequisite for service on a district group. Parents demonstrate their commitment and gain valuable experience prior to becoming district representatives.

# E. Train Parents and Staff

Intensive training for parent and staff members of advisory groups is a key feature separating successful from unsuccessful advisory groups. Well-conceived training programs accomplish several purposes for districts seeking active advisory groups. First, participants develop important skills and receive useful substantive and procedural information. For example, members must understand the selection and recruitment standards for district employees before participating in personnel decision making. Second, training programs imbue parents (especially inexperienced parents) with a sense of confidence about their potential contributions to the advisory group. For example, a training program on reading a budget reveals to parents that they are quite capable of making sense out of the tangle of figures. Third, training components devoted to leadership development ensure that the advisory group will have an energetic core of leaders.

Both preservice and inservice training efforts are advisable. Preservice training enables parents and staff to function efficiently in the advisory group right from the outset. Inservice training is tailored to deal with the solution of recurring problems, since by then participants understand well the areas in which they need the most help.

Although the training practices that follow address the entire advisory group, they are equally applicable if your advisory group is organized into multiple subcommittees. No matter which of the practices you use, plan on periodic assessment to determine whether your training program continues to respond to the real needs of members.

## What Works: Successful Practices

### ■ Membership Training

Training sessions for the entire membership are held during the beginning of the school year and at critical points throughout the year. Topics include:

—advisory group role and objectives;

—state/district policies and practices;

—decision area information seminars (for example, on budget or curriculum);

—effective group processes;

—good decision making.

Sessions are conducted by district personnel, consultants from a local university or other organization, or by the most experienced members of the advisory group.

### ■ Leadership Training

Most parents need guidance in fulfilling a leadership role in an active, policy-oriented group. Preservice sessions are held for newly elected advisory group officers, while inservice efforts are directed to officers who have been on the job for a while. Valuable topics include:

—conducting a meeting, including the use of parliamentary procedures;

—establishing communication channels;

—setting up an agenda;

—managing a small group;

—using effective problem-solving techniques.

Opportunities for on-the-job leadership training also exist. For example, inexperienced parents can exercise leadership within subcommittees, which are smaller and more manageable than the whole advisory group.

### ■ Information Exchanges

Successful practices are shared among functioning advisory groups. Consultation with older advisory groups often eliminates having to learn by making the same mistakes. Regional and state workshops are also good vehicles for information exchange. In addition, representatives from successful groups can be brought in as short-term consultants to provide inservice technical assistance in a given area.

■ Informal Sharing of Experiences

Veteran advisors or members share their wisdom and experience in informal conversations with newer members. These conversations provide invaluable information to new members, especially during the initial stages of service when they do not yet "know the ropes."

# F. Establish Communication Channels

Advisory groups that participate in decision making depend on having members who are well informed about district policies, the day-to-day operations of the schools and advisory group business. It is, therefore, important to establish communication channels within the advisory group and between the group and the schools. Further, if an advisory group is meant to be a liaison between parents and the schools, advisory group members must maintain considerable contact with the parent community. To be sensitive to the needs and concerns of the parent population demands frequent and honest communication.

In many districts, advisory group members communicate well among themselves but are isolated from both the parents and the schools. Not only do these groups lack the information and insights to participate in serious decision making, but few people in the school system even know that they exist. When, on the other hand, advisory groups communicate extensively with the outside environment, their members feel knowledgeable and valued.

Below we discuss a variety of practices for communicating effectively. With your advisory group, try to use several of these practices in combination to satisfy communications needs.

## What Works: Successful Practices

■ Frequent Advisory Group Meetings

Well-run meetings give advisory group members the opportunity to communicate among themselves. To maximize this opportunity, you need to consider seriously the time, place and duration of meetings. Each of these elements should be negotiated to determine what will be convenient for the greatest number of members.

In addition, structuring meetings carefully will contribute to good attendance and the quality of communication. An agenda ought to be prepared and distributed (by the coordinator or chairperson) in advance of each meeting so that members know what topics will be discussed.

Ample time should be built into meetings for open discussions among members and attendees about topics introduced. Many districts also set up separate discussion groups composed of parents and district personnel who meet to debate major issues, such as program monitoring in the schools. Reports are then made to the entire advisory group.

### ■ School Staff Presentations

One way that an advisory group that has decision-making responsibilities can keep informed about district operations is to hear periodic presentations from district staff. For example, the district supervisor of instructional programs talks to the group about plans for introducing a pilot social studies program at three elementary schools. Time is provided for members to ask questions and comment on the plans. This method for staying informed should be combined with firsthand observations so that members get a balanced view of district operations.

### ■ Firsthand Observations

Visiting ongoing programs in the schools affords advisory group members the chance to observe for themselves the operations about which they help make decisions. They are also able to communicate directly with the teachers who are responsible for implementing district programs. These visits inform parents about what is going well with the programs and what problems teachers are facing.

### ■ Attendance at School Board Meetings

The school board is the major policy-making body in any district. If an advisory group is to participate in decision making, then it should set up communication channels between itself and the school board. One way is to have an advisory group representative regularly attend board meetings. This person takes notes on issues discussed, reports back to the advisory group and can, when appropriate, present the advisory group's position on an issue to the board.

### ■ Subcommittee Reports

If your advisory group uses a subcommittee structure, you should be sure that the subcommittees communicate periodically with the entire advisory group. Building in time at large-group meetings for subcommittee progress reports is a good idea. Similarly, before voting on any issue for which a subcommittee is responsible, the advisory group should seek a thorough presentation of all alternatives from the subcommittee leadership.

### ■ Distribution of Materials

Calendars and notices are circulated to announce meeting times, dates and activities of the advisory group. To keep parents informed and interested, copies of meeting minutes are distributed to all members and to all parent non-members who have attended at least one meeting. Minutes are also filed in a central district location so they are available to any interested person. Materials will have to be translated into another language in those districts where substantial numbers of parents do not have a command of English.

### ■ Media

Reporters from local newspapers are invited to attend and report on important meetings so that the public is informed about advisory group activities. The names of members in attendance can also be publicized in these articles serving as an extra incentive to parents.

In addition, public access television is available in many communities. Videotape coverage of important advisory group meetings is thereby provided.

■ **Social Interaction**
The advisory group sponsors social gatherings where members are able to talk informally with parents and educators about the goals and activities of the group. A potluck dinner is one such gathering. It's particularly effective at the beginning of the school year to introduce new members to old members and to inform all members about the concerns and interests of parents. You can also plan social hours after group meetings, where attendees converse over coffee and cake. Many of the meeting's topics will carry right into the social hour.

# G. Support Ongoing Activities

Advisory groups that can count on basic support services are more successful in meeting their goals and objectives. The provision of support services by districts seems to have two kinds of impacts. First, the services are often essential in enabling the groups to carry on business. Second, the services carry with them an implicit message to advisory groups that their activities are considered important to district operations.

## Provide Services and Supplies

Involvement in an active advisory group demands both time and energy from parents. Some parents, especially those with young children and limited incomes, have to make significant personal sacrifices to participate fully. By providing services and supplies, you can ensure that entire segments of the parent community won't exclude themselves from advisory group participation because of the personal hardship involved.

## What Works: Successful Practices

■ **Babysitting or Child Care**
Districts provide child-care services for children of advisory group members while meetings are taking place. Or, they encourage parents to form cooperative child-care arrangements where one parent takes care of several children in a room in the school while their parents are attending a meeting in another room. If the district has no funds for child care, you may want to help the advisory group plan fundraisers.

■ Transportation

Providing assistance with transportation or reimbursement for mileage enables parents to attend meetings and perform other advisory group tasks. For those parents who don't have a car or access to public transportation, the chairperson circulates a list of the names and addresses of members. Ride-sharing may also appeal to parents who wish to economize on fuel costs.

■ Documents

A variety of written materials are made available for advisory group reference. These resource materials include: (1) federal, state and local program guidelines and regulations; (2) district and state program summaries; (3) program handbooks; and (4) announcements, newsletters, agendas. It is a good idea to keep these materials in a central location where members and other interested parties can have easy access to them.

■ Clerical Services and Supplies

Services such as typing, printing and mailing are provided by the district. Frequently, the advisory group coordinator is the key person in securing such support.

To recruit parents who are not fluent in English, translating services are necessary. On going translations of proceedings may also be necessary at group meetings.

■ Recognition

The morale of advisory group members is sustained by recognition of their services. An annual luncheon or banquet honoring the advisory group is one way to extend appreciation. Another way is to recognize the individual contributions of members by having a "member of the year" award.

Coverage of advisory group activities by the local media is another form of recognition. People enjoy seeing their names and ideas in the newspaper or on television.

## Monitor and Evaluate

Periodically, the coordinator and chairperson should take stock of advisory group operations, looking for ways of improving the nature and extent of participation in decision making. This evaluation can take place on a formal or informal basis. But, at very least, the membership ought to be asked about their perceptions of areas that need improvement and strategies that might work well.

## What Works: Successful Practices

■ Self-Assessment

At six-month intervals, the advisory group coordinator and chairperson assess the degree to which the group is meeting its goals and objectives. In formal interviews or informal conversations, they ask members and other regular attendees (including district administrators) for their opinions about the activities of the group and the ways in which improvements could be achieved.

An alternative is to develop brief questionnaires to tap the same information. Questionnaires are of course sent out to more respondents than can be interviewed.

### ■ Consultant Review

For those districts that have some money in their advisory group budget, an outside consultant is brought in to study group operations and make recommendations about possible improvements. This consultant should have a proven track record of having helped advisory groups in the past. Once invited, the consultant is given access to all group documents, files, members and meetings.

## Examples of Success

In our study, we saw many advisory groups that were making significant contributions to district or school decision making. Below are brief profiles of two such groups.

### Point School Advisory Committee

The Point advisory committee was active in almost every phase of the school's educational program. The chairperson had a desk in an office near the principal's and was in the school all day each day. She therefore was a regular participant in ongoing discussions among school staff, acting as the advisory committee's representative. She also noted issues that she wanted to bring to the committee's attention. Beyond this ongoing involvement, the Point advisory committee also helped formulate each year's master plan and participated in all personnel decisions. Finally, the advisory committee had sole responsibility for decisions about the parental involvement program, including parent education activities, field trips, cultural events, etc.

The advisory committee met monthly in the school's parent room. Agendas were set by, and the meetings conducted exclusively by, the chairperson. Staff and paraprofessionals attended these meetings along with parent members. Training for members was extensive and included regular monthly training sessions put on by district staff, local university consultants and community representatives. Subjects ranged from the role of the advisory committee to parental rights. In addition, some members went each spring to a state-sponsored workshop with other advisory committees.

### Valhalla District Advisory Committee

The Valhalla advisory committee, consisting of 20 parent members, was organized into an elaborate subcommittee structure. The subcommittees included: the Personnel Committee, the Site Transportation Committee and the Political Action Committee. The advisory committee participated in decision making both independently and in conjunction with district staff. It functioned autonomously when it: located school sites to house various district programs; raised funds for an advisory committee budget and controlled its own expenditures (in the neighborhood of $5,000); actively recruited parents to help out with advisory committee-sponsored activities; and interviewed and hired district aides. It worked with district staff when it interviewed and recommended applicants for teaching positions, reviewed and suggested instructional curriculum materials and advised on budget allocations.

The entire advisory committee met at least four times annually. The subcommittees met on an as-needed basis and reported their activities regularly to the whole group. Meetings were conducted and agendas set exclusively by parent members.

# PART II

## *The Self-Assessment Manual*

# The Self-Assessment Manual

*The Self-Assessment Manual (SAM) can be used by anyone responsible for involving parents in the education of children. It has two basic purposes: (1) to help you evaluate your present parental involvement activities; and (2) to help you diagnose problem areas in these activities so that you can plan improvements. To accomplish these purposes, SAM first helps you prepare a profile of your parental involvement program that will show graphically where your efforts have succeeded and where you may want to improve. After interpreting the profile, you will complete a checklist that should aid you in planning any improvements. Finally, you will fill out a form that will serve as an action plan for your efforts.*

*SAM grows directly out of Part I: How to Set Up Parental Involvement Activities. The two parts are meant to be used hand-in-hand, with SAM guiding your use of Part I. SAM uses criteria for success and vital ingredients discussed in Chapters 3-7. It leads you through a systematic evaluation of your program based on these sections of Part I. Because of their close relationship, we have suggested that you become familiar with Part I before starting the self-assessment process.*

*SAM is divided into five sections, each corresponding to one of the parental involvement components in Part I (school support, parent education, etc.). You will find that each of the sections contains similar materials—one Profile Worksheet, one or two brief impact questionnaires, one Vital Ingredients Checklist and one Planning Form.*

*Before going on to any of the five sections, read the next section entitled "How to Use SAM" carefully. It will explain the self-assessment process in considerable detail.*

# How to Use
# SAM

The self-assessment process consists of four steps that are explained below. As you read, keep in mind that self-assessment ought to be an ongoing process. You will probably want to use SAM materials more than once, as you move into cycles of assessing activities at Time 1, improving them and assessing them again at Time 2.

## Step 1—
## Develop the Parent Involvement Profile

On page 102 you will find the Parent Involvement Profile, on which you will describe graphically how well your district is doing in the full range of parental involvement components. For each component, the Parent Involvement Profile lists, in a shorthand fashion, the criteria for success presented in the handbook. Next to the criteria are scales. For example, the first criterion in the School Support area is "% Parents Participating"; next to it is a scale running from 0 to 100%.

To complete the scales for a given component, use the Profile Worksheet and impact questionnaires found in the corresponding section of SAM. The worksheet is designed to ask questions derived from the criteria for success. After answering these questions on the worksheet, transfer your answers to the appropriate scale on the Parent Involvement Profile. **Remember that the criteria for success and related scales represent ideals toward which a parental involvement program can strive. They are not absolute standards that you either attain or** don't attain. In fact you may be confronted with circumstances in your project that make it unrealistic to even establish a particular criterion as a long-term goal.

Most worksheet items are straightforward, factual questions that can probably be answered by you or your staff; on occasion, you may want to seek help from others who might be better acquainted with the component.

The worksheet items on impacts are different. We believe that the best way to assess impacts is through surveying those people who might have firsthand experience—staff and parents. Therefore, each section of SAM contains a page from one or more questionnaires (usually a parent questionnaire and a teacher questionnaire).* For example, the School Support section contains a page from a Parent Questionnaire and a page from a Teacher Questionnaire. You can take the questionnaire pages from each section and put together a parent survey instrument and a staff survey instrument.

The results from these surveys can be used in a variety of ways: they will produce interesting, relevant information. For the limited purpose of filling out the Parent Involvement Profile, we ask that you calculate average scores and transfer them to the appropriate scales on the Parent Involvement Profile. Directions for these calculations are presented on the Profile Worksheets.

# Step 2—
# Interpret the Parent Involvement Profile

By studying the completed Parent Involvement Profile, you will be able to determine which components of your program could stand some improvement. You should not feel that meeting each criterion is a win or lose proposition. If, for example, only 50% of the classrooms in your project have a parent instructional aide (Criterion 1: School Instructional Aides), you haven't lost. Rather, you've identified an area in which you might be able to improve and set a higher standard for your operations. Depending on conditions at your site, you may eventually set a goal (Step 4) of increasing the percentage of classrooms having parent aides to 60% by next year. Or, given those conditions, you may conclude that 50% is as high as you can go.

For those components where improvement is necessary and possible, you should move on to Step 3 of the assessment process.

---

* The exception is the section on advisory groups. It does not contain a questionnaire page.

# Step 3—
# Complete the Vital Ingredients Checklist

If you want to improve your program (whether a lot or a little), the handbook can help. As we have said, completing the Vital Ingredients Checklist will assist you in using the handbook to best advantage.

Part I describes the seven ingredients that are vital to the success of parental involvement in any component. In the Vital Ingredients Checklist for a component, we repeat the seven basic ingredients and provide a list of action steps that need to be taken to mix the ingredients into your operations. For each of the "vital ingredients"—no matter what component is being assessed—we recommend the following procedures:

- Read the statements related to the ingredient and place a check by those that describe accurately steps you have already taken.
- If you are able to check all of the statements, then move on to the next "vital ingredient."
- If you are unable to check a statement, then look carefully through the pages that are referenced in the far right-hand column of the checklist.

These are the pages of Part I of the handbook that contain information related to that action step, including actual practices and strategies that have worked well for educators around the country who wanted effective parent involvement programs.

Please note that in addition to the action steps laid out in Part I, we have left space for you to write in any step that you deem necessary because of local circumstances.

Having filled out the Vital Ingredients Checklist and reviewed the appropriate sections of Part I, you are probably ready to plan actual improvements for your program. Step 4 will help you do so.

# Step 4—
# Fill Out the Parental Involvement Planning Form

This form will enable you to plan systematically the improvements you need to make in any parental involvement activity area, based on insights and ideas from Steps 1-3 in the self-assessment process. We recommend that you establish plans for three-month blocks of time.

By reexamining the Parent Involvement Profile, you will be in a position to set goals. Simply put, this involves determining where you are on the profile for a criterion and where you want to be. For example, if the profile indicates that 30% of your parents participate in school-support activities, you may decide that a goal of increasing that rate of participation to 50% is feasible and desirable.

The next column on the form is the place to list objectives designed to accomplish the overall goal. Here the Vital Ingredients Checklist will assist. Those checklist action steps that you have not yet satisfied can be listed in the "Objectives" column of the form. For example, an objective in meeting the goal of increasing participation in school support from 30% to 50% might be to develop a new recruitment strategy.

Next the objectives need to be translated into a series of specific tasks. You'll be able to get some ideas for defining these tasks from the practices and strategies described in the "What Works: Successful Practices" sections of Part I. To follow through with our example, Task I associated with your objective of developing a new recruitment strategy might be to have two parent members from the district advisory group write a monthly newsletter describing upcoming activities for which parent volunteers are needed.

Finally, after establishing goals, objectives and tasks designed to improve your program, you should decide on reasonable target dates for completion. There are no simple guidelines that we can offer for setting target dates; the amount of time that it will take to implement any element in your plan will depend greatly on local factors, such as resources at your disposal.

**One thing to keep in mind: After implementing changes in your program, use SAM again after the changes have had a chance to germinate.**

# Figure 1. The Self-Assessment Process

**STEP 1**

Develop the Parental
Involvement Profile

• Decide what components
you want to assess.

• Conduct parent and staff
surveys for these components.

• Score questionnaires and
transfer scores to Profile
Worksheets and Profile.

• Complete Profile Work-
sheets for these components
and transfer information to
Profile.

**STEP 2**

Interpret the Parental
Involvement Profile

• Determine from the
Profile which components
you want to improve.

• Decide whether improve-
ments are possible for these
components.

• For components where
improvement is necessary
and possible, go on to
Step 3.

**STEP 3**

Complete the Vital
Ingredients Checklist

• Read all statements for
an ingredient.

• Check statements that
describe your operations.

• If all statements are
checked, go on to the next
ingredient.

• If all statements are not
checked, read the references
for that Ingredient in Part 1
and go on to Step 4.

**STEP 4**

Fill Out the
Planning Form

• By reexamining the
Profile, establish reasonable
goals for a component.

• Identify action steps from
the Checklist that are objectives in meeting your goal.

• Define specific tasks
associated with these
objectives.

• Set target dates for
implementing your plan of
action.

# PARENT INVOLVEMENT PROFILE

**INVOLVING PARENTS IN:**

## SCHOOL SUPPORT

| | 0 | | | | 50% | | | 100% |
|---|---|---|---|---|---|---|---|---|
| % Parents Participating | 0 | | | | 50% | | | 100% |
| # Activities | 0 | | | | 5 | | | 10+ |

| | 1 | 1.5 | 2.0 | 2.5 | 3.0 | 3.5 | 4.0 |
|---|---|---|---|---|---|---|---|
| Impacts: Parents | 1 | 1.5 | 2.0 | 2.5 | 3.0 | 3.5 | 4.0 |
| Impacts: Teachers | 1 | 1.5 | 2.0 | 2.5 | 3.0 | 3.5 | 4.0 |

## PARENT EDUCATION

| | 0 | | | | 50% | | | 100% |
|---|---|---|---|---|---|---|---|---|
| % Parents Participating | 0 | | | | 50% | | | 100% |
| % Targeted | 0 | | | | 50% | | | 100% |
| Impacts: Parents | 1 | 1.5 | 2.0 | 2.5 | 3.0 | 3.5 | 4 |

## HOME-BASED INSTRUCTION

| | 0 | | | | 50% | | | 100% |
|---|---|---|---|---|---|---|---|---|
| % Parents Participating | 0 | | | | 50% | | | 100% |
| Impacts: Parents | 1 | 1.5 | 2.0 | 2.5 | 3.0 | 3.5 | 4 |
| Impacts: Teachers | 1 | 1.5 | 2.0 | 2.5 | 3.0 | 3.5 | 4 |

## INSTRUCTION AT SCHOOL

| | 0 | | | | 50% | | | 100% |
|---|---|---|---|---|---|---|---|---|
| % Classrooms | 0 | | | | 50% | | | 100% |
| % Time on Instruction | 0 | | | | 50% | | | 100% |
| % Planning Instruction | 0 | | | | 50% | | | 100% |
| % Regular | 0 | | | | 50% | | | 100% |
| Impacts: Parents | 1 | 1.5 | 2.0 | 2.5 | 3.0 | 3.5 | 4 |
| Impacts: Teachers | 1 | 1.5 | 2.0 | 2.5 | 3.0 | 3.5 | 4 |

## ADVISORY GROUPS

| | No Involvement | Inform Only | Minor Role | Major Role |
|---|---|---|---|---|
| Role: Curriculum | No Involvement | Inform Only | Minor Role | Major Role |
| Role: Budget | No Involvement | Inform Only | Minor Role | Major Role |
| Role: Personnel | No Involvement | Inform Only | Minor Role | Major Role |
| Role: Parent Activities | No Involvement | Inform Only | Minor Role | Major Role |

# Profile Worksheet: Involving Parents in School Support

The handbook defines successful school support as follows: Most parents should be involved in at least one activity that contributes to the economic, political or moral support of the school. There are three aspects to this definition of success. Paraphrased from the handbook, they are:

1. It is important for *most parents* to help, to obtain and demonstrate broad-based support. Unless many people participate in some way, it is less likely that your goals will be met. Responsibility will rest on a few shoulders, and those few individuals may burn out and leave a leadership gap.

2. Participation *in at least one activity* is an attainable goal. Most parents work, so they have limited time to provide services or resources to schools. But, since many school-support activities are of short duration and have very specific goals, they provide opportunities for parents who are only able to make short-term commitments.

3. *"Contributes to the economic, political and moral support of the school"* means that support activities are important to a school's continued functioning. Schools always require moral support—parents who are willing to express belief in the school's objectives and goals—and occasionally they require economic and political support. Parents can contribute to resources a school budget can't allow. Support from parents can influence decision makers to keep alive special programs.

## Judging the Status of Your School-Support Program

The questions below are based on the three statements imbedded in the criterion for success. Answer them here and then transfer your answers to the corresponding scales on the profile.

1. WHAT PERCENTAGE OF PARENTS PARTICIPATE AT ALL IN SCHOOL-SUPPORT ACTIVITIES? (% Parents Participating)

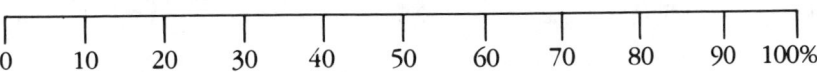

0   10   20   30   40   50   60   70   80   90   100%

2. HOW MANY DIFFERENT SCHOOL-SUPPORT ACTIVITIES DO YOU HAVE DURING THE SCHOOL YEAR? (# of Activities)

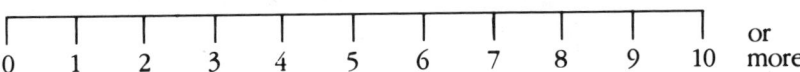

0   1   2   3   4   5   6   7   8   9   10   or more

To complete the next two items, use the results from the school-support sections of the Parent and Teacher Questionnaires. Follow these steps:

1. Compute the AVERAGE RATING for *each* questionnaire.

   Add all the ratings on a questionnaire. Write the total at the bottom. Divide the total you just got by the number of items. Write that number (for example, 2.5), the average rating, at the bottom.

2. Compute the TOTAL RATINGS for *all* questionnaires.

   (a) Add all Parent Questionnaire average ratings.
   (b) Count the number of Parent Questionnaires.
   (c) Divide the total by the number of questionnaires.

   TOTAL: _____
   NO. QUESTIONNAIRES: _____
   TOTAL RATING: _____
   (Parents)

   ...............................................................

   (a) Add all Teacher Questionnaire average ratings.
   (b) Count the number of Teacher Questionnaires.
   (c) Divide the total by the number of questionnaires.

   TOTAL: _____
   NO. QUESTIONNAIRES: _____
   TOTAL RATING: _____
   (Teachers)

3. WHAT CONTRIBUTIONS HAS THE SCHOOL-SUPPORT PROGRAM HAD, ACCORDING TO PARENTS? (Impacts: Parents)

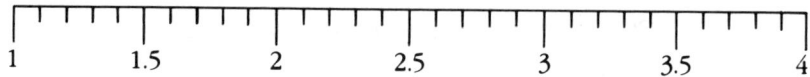

1     1.5     2     2.5     3     3.5     4

4. WHAT CONTRIBUTIONS HAS THE SCHOOL-SUPPORT PROGRAM HAD, ACCORDING TO TEACHERS? (Impacts: Teachers)

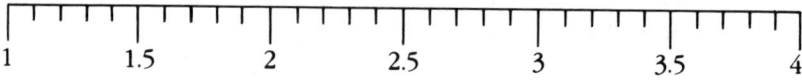

1     1.5     2     2.5     3     3.5     4

# PARENT QUESTIONNAIRE: SCHOOL-SUPPORT SECTION

_____ I have volunteered to help at the school, or at home, but not as a classroom volunteer. Classroom volunteering will be covered in another section of this questionnaire. (Answer questions below.)

_____ I have not volunteered to help at the school. (Please go on to the next page.)

---

### HOW DO YOU FEEL ABOUT THE STATEMENTS BELOW?
#### (Circle your choice.)

| | Strongly Agree | Agree | Disagree | Strongly Disagree |
|---|---|---|---|---|
| 1. Parent volunteers have provided useful items that are used in the school's programs. | 4 | 3 | 2 | 1 |
| 2. Parent volunteers have raised money that the school needs for its programs. | 4 | 3 | 2 | 1 |
| 3. Parent volunteers who write letters or speak to officials have helped keep school programs alive. | 4 | 3 | 2 | 1 |
| 4. Parent volunteers have supported the school's goals. | 4 | 3 | 2 | 1 |
| 5. Parent volunteers have supported the school's programs. | 4 | 3 | 2 | 1 |

---

Total Ratings: _____ No. Items: _____ Average Rating: _____

# TEACHER QUESTIONNAIRE: SCHOOL-SUPPORT SECTION

HOW DO YOU FEEL ABOUT THE STATEMENTS BELOW?
(Circle your choice.)

| | Strongly Agree | Agree | Disagree | Strongly Disagree |
|---|---|---|---|---|
| 1. Parent volunteers have provided useful items that are used in the school's programs. | 4 | 3 | 2 | 1 |
| 2. Parent volunteers have raised money that the school needs for its programs. | 4 | 3 | 2 | 1 |
| 3. Parent volunteers who write letters or speak to officials have helped keep school programs alive. | 4 | 3 | 2 | 1 |
| 4. Parent volunteers have supported the school's goals. | 4 | 3 | 2 | 1 |
| 5. Parent volunteers have supported the school's programs. | 4 | 3 | 2 | 1 |

Total Ratings: _____ No. Items: ___5___ Average Rating: _____

# VITAL INGREDIENTS CHECKLIST

| VITAL INGREDIENT | | ACTION STEPS | PAGE NO. |
|---|---|---|---|
| PROVIDE COORDINATION FOR ACTIVITIES | | Assign a person(s) at the district or school level to be responsible for: (a) arranging each school-support activity; (b) coordinating activities so that they do not conflict with other programs or activities in the school or district; (c) assessing school needs and parent resources; (d) recruiting parents; (e) providing necessary support services and supplies. | 11 22* |
| | | (Space for Local Action Steps) | |
| ASSESS NEEDS AND RESOURCES | | Conduct a formal or informal assessment of school needs. | 11 24* |
| | | Conduct a formal or informal assessment of what parents can and will do. | 11 24* |
| | | Match school needs and parent resources. | 11 24* |
| | | (Space for Local Action Steps) | |
| SPECIFY AND COMMUNICATE PARENT ROLES | | Clearly specify what roles parent volunteers will and will not have in the school. | 13 25* |
| | | Involve parents, teachers and staff in agreeing on parent volunteer roles. | 13 25* |
| | | Communicate the agreed-upon roles to potential parent volunteers. | 14 26* |
| | | (Space for Local Action Steps) | |
| RECRUIT, SELECT AND ASSIGN PARENT VOLUNTEERS | | Develop a variety of recruitment strategies for attracting parent volunteers to the school. | 14 27* |
| | | Develop procedures for matching volunteers' skills with school needs. | 14 27* |
| | | (Space for Local Action Steps) | |
| TRAIN PARENTS AND STAFF | | When the activity requires it, provide training for volunteers in: (a) relevant school rules and policies; (b) information necessary for the particular activity (for example, background information for a field trip, travel arrangements and so forth). | 28* |

* Handbook reference for "What Works: Successful Practices" relating to action steps.

# VITAL INGREDIENTS CHECKLIST

| VITAL INGREDIENT | √ | ACTION STEPS | PAGE NO. |
|---|---|---|---|
| TRAIN PARENTS AND STAFF (continued) | | Provide training for school staff on how to use volunteers most effectively. | 28* |
| | | Plan training on the basis of formal and informal assessments of volunteer and staff needs. | 16 |
| | | Provide at least some training for staff and parents together. | 29* |
| | | Evaluate mechanisms for communication between parents and staff about school-support activities. | 16 |
| | | (Space for Local Action Steps) | |
| ESTABLISH COMMUNICATION CHANNELS | | Establish mechanisms for communication between parents and staff about school-support activities. | 16 29* |
| | | Establish mechanisms for communication among parent volunteers. | 17 30* |
| | | (Space for Local Action Steps) | |
| SUPPORT ONGOING ACTIVITIES | | Provide material services or supplies that will make it easier for them to volunteer. | 18 30* |
| | | Recognize and reward the contributions of individual parent volunteers. | 18 32* |
| | | Establish procedures for carefully monitoring the school-support program, in order to demonstrate its importance and to tell whether assignments for aides need to be revised, whether more or fewer volunteers are needed and whether those already participating think it is worthwhile. | 18 32* |
| | | (Space for Local Action Steps) | |

* Handbook reference for "What Works: Successful Practices" relating to action steps.

# PARENTAL INVOLVEMENT PLANNING FORM

| | GOALS (PROFILE) | OBJECTIVES (VITAL INGREDIENTS/ ACTION STEPS) | TASKS | TARGET COMPLETION DATES |
|---|---|---|---|---|
| 3 MO | | | | |
| 6 MO | | | | |
| 9 MO | | | | |
| 1 YR | | | | |

# Profile Worksheet: Involving Parents in Parent Education

The handbook presents three criteria for judging the success of your parental involvement in parent education programs.

1. *It ensures that a majority of parents participate in at least one activity.* This is another way of saying that most parents want to participate. This does not mean that a majority participates in any one activity, but rather the total set of activities is diverse enough to appeal to the interests of most parents.

2. *It is targeted to the needs of parents of children in the school.* A parent education component must focus on real wants and needs of parents. If not, few parents will participate. Matching activities to needs goes beyond responding to just a core group of parents. It means finding out what parents in general want and providing activities that are of popular interest, such as drug abuse seminars and parenting workshops. Or it means designing programs targeted to the specific needs of individual parents, such as English as a second language, general education courses (GED), jewelry making and foreign languages.

3. *Parents feel that they learn something of value.* The ultimate measure of the success of a parent education component is that parents feel that they have learned something useful. Learning can be quite concrete: for example, the acquisition of a new skill such as knitting or dancing. Or learning may be more subjective: for example, a feeling of greater confidence when dealing with public agencies. Either way, it is primarily parents themselves who are able to determine the value of parent education offerings.

## Judging the Status of Your Parent Education Program

The questions that follow are based on the three criteria for success repeated above. Answer them here and then transfer your answers to the corresponding scales on the profile.

1. WHAT PERCENTAGE OF PARENTS HAVE PARTICIPATED IN AT LEAST ONE PARENT EDUCATION WORKSHOP OR ACTIVITY? (% Parents Participating)

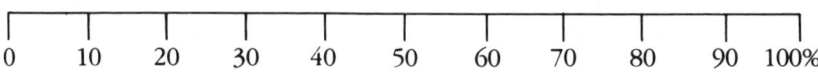

| 0 | 10 | 20 | 30 | 40 | 50 | 60 | 70 | 80 | 90 | 100% |

2. WHAT PERCENTAGE OF THE PARENT EDUCATION WORKSHOPS, MATERIALS OR ACTIVITIES DURING THE PAST YEAR WERE PLANNED ON THE BASIS OF FORMAL OR INFORMAL ASSESSMENTS OF PARENTS' NEEDS AND DESIRES? (% Targeted)

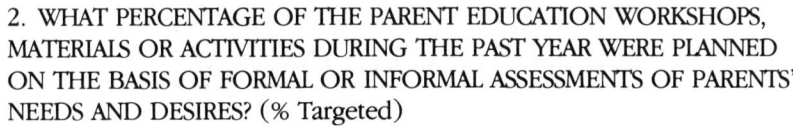

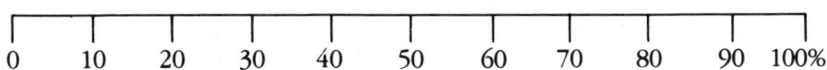

To complete the next item, use the results from the parent education section of the Parent Questionnaire, following these steps:

1. Compute the AVERAGE RATING for *each* questionnaire.

   Add all the ratings on a questionnaire. Write the total at the bottom. Divide the total you just got by the number of items. Write that number—the average rating—at the bottom.

2. Compute the TOTAL RATING for all questionnaires.

   (a) Add all Parent Questionnaire average ratings.
   (b) Count the number of Parent Questionnaires returned.
   (c) Divide the total by the number of questionnaires.

   TOTAL: _____
   NO. QUESTIONNAIRES: _____
   TOTAL RATING: _____
   (Parents)

3. WHAT IMPACT HAS THE PARENT EDUCATION PROGRAM HAD, ACCORDING TO PARENTS? (Impacts: Parents)

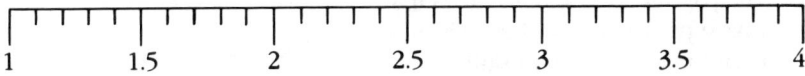

# PARENT QUESTIONNAIRE: PARENT EDUCATION SECTION

Have you attended any "parent education" or "adult education" workshops or activities at your child's school (for example, sewing or cooking classes, "parenting" workshops, nutrition programs or general education classes)?

Yes _____     (Please write the name of the class or activities below.)

_____

_____

_____

_____

No _____     (Please go to the next page.)

---

### HOW DO YOU FEEL ABOUT THE STATEMENTS BELOW?
#### (Circle your choice.)

|  | Strongly Agree | Agree | Disagree | Strongly Disagree |
|---|---|---|---|---|
| 1. The parent education activities that I have participated in have given me useful information and skills. | 4 | 3 | 2 | 1 |
| 2. Parent education activities have helped make parents more aware of the school and supportive of its programs. | 4 | 3 | 2 | 1 |

---

Total Ratings: _____ No. Items: ___2___ Average Rating: _____

# VITAL INGREDIENTS CHECKLIST

| VITAL INGREDIENT | √ | ACTION STEPS | PAGE NO. |
|---|---|---|---|
| PROVIDE COORDINATION FOR ACTIVITIES | | Assign a person(s) at the district or school level to be responsible for:<br>(a) assessing parent needs;<br>(b) finding outside resources;<br>(c) providing necessary support services and supplies;<br>(d) arranging and publicizing activities. | 11<br>36* |
| | | (Space for Local Action Steps) | |
| ASSESS NEEDS AND RESOURCES | | Conduct formal or informal assessments of all parents' needs and desires for parent education activities and materials. | 11<br>37* |
| | | Use the findings from these assessments to plan parent education activities, workshops and materials targeted to parents' expressed needs. | 11<br>38* |
| | | Identify which parent education resources are available in the community already and which will have to be supplied by the school. | 11<br>38* |
| | | (Space for Local Action Steps) | |
| SPECIFY AND COMMUNICATE PARENT ROLES | | Formally or informally specify a role for parents as teachers and learners. | 13<br>40* |
| | | Communicate the agreed-upon role to parents through handbooks or meetings to make them aware of what opportunities are open to them. | 13<br>40* |
| | | Involve parents, teachers and administrators in defining and agreeing upon these roles. | 13 |
| | | (Space for Local Action Steps) | |
| RECRUIT AND ASSIGN PARENT PARTICIPANTS | | Develop recruitment strategies that inform parents about activities and interest them in participating. | 14<br>41* |
| | | If languages other than English are used in the community, translate recruitment literature into those languages. | 41*<br>42* |
| | | Announce activities well in advance so parents can arrange their schedules. | 41* |
| | | (Space for Local Action Steps) | |

\* Handbook reference for "What Works: Successful Practices" relating to the action steps.

# VITAL INGREDIENTS CHECKLIST

| VITAL INGREDIENT | | ACTION STEPS | PAGE NO. |
|---|---|---|---|
| TRAIN STAFF | | If the workshop presenter has not worked with parents before, work with him/her to sensitize him/her to the needs and concerns of parents. | 15 42* |
| | | (Space for Local Action Steps) | |
| ESTABLISH COMMUNI-CATION CHANNELS | | Establish channels for parents to communicate to staff their needs and desires for parent education activities. | 16 43* |
| | | Establish procedures for parents to evaluate parent education activities and suggest ways to improve them. | 16 43* |
| | | (Space for Local Action Steps) | |
| SUPPORT ONGOING ACTIVITIES | | Offer parents material services or supplies (such as transportation, child care, tuition or materials) that will make it easier for them to participate in parent education activities. | 18 44* |
| | | (Space for Local Action Steps) | |

\* Handbook reference for "What Works: Successful Practices" relating to action steps.

# PARENTAL INVOLVEMENT PLANNING FORM

|  | GOALS (PROFILE) | OBJECTIVES (VITAL INGREDIENTS/ ACTION STEPS) | TASKS | TARGET COMPLETION DATES |
|---|---|---|---|---|
| 3 MO |  |  |  |  |
| 6 MO |  |  |  |  |
| 9 MO |  |  |  |  |
| 1 YR |  |  |  |  |

# Profile Worksheet:
# Involving Parents in Home-Based Instruction

The handbook presents two criteria for judging the success of your parental involvement in home-based instruction.

1. *It involves most parents in at least one activity.* Parental participation in this area is really a continuation of what parents already do with their children at home. The range of possible activities should be broad enough, and requirements flexible enough, to suit the differences in parental interest level and available time. Most parents can benefit from suggestions for helping their children in some area.

2. *It has positive results for the child.* While it may be difficult to link increases in achievement test scores to the help that students receive at home, there are other effects of successful home assistance that can be traced. Students whose parents help them at home not only learn more, but they also have more positive attitudes toward learning. Attendance is better, students feel more comfortable with classwork and they come to school with greater confidence when parents actively support the learning process at home.

## Judging the Status of Your Home-Based Instruction Program

The questions that follow are based on the two criteria for success repeated above. Answer them here and then transfer your answers to the corresponding scales on the profile.

1. WHAT PERCENTAGE OF PARENTS HAVE PARTICIPATED IN AT LEAST ONE ACTIVITY SPONSORED BY THE SCHOOL TO ENCOURAGE HOME-BASED INSTRUCTION? (% Parents Participating)

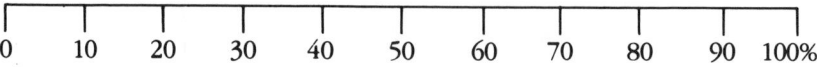

| 0 | 10 | 20 | 30 | 40 | 50 | 60 | 70 | 80 | 90 | 100% |

To complete the next two items, use the results from the home-based instruction sections of the questionnaires. Follow these steps:

1. Compute the AVERAGE RATING for *each* questionnaire.

   Add all the ratings on a questionnaire. Write the total at the bottom. Divide the total you just got by the number of items. Write that number—the average rating—at the bottom.

2. Compute the TOTAL RATINGS for *all* questionnaires.

   (a) Add all Parent Questionnaire average ratings.
   (b) Count the number of Parent Questionnaires.
   (c) Divide the total by the number of questionnaires.

   TOTAL: _____
   NO. QUESTIONNAIRES: _____
   TOTAL RATING: _____
   (Parents)

   (a) Add all Teacher Questionnaire average ratings.
   (b) Count the number of Teacher Questionnaires.
   (c) Divide the total by the number of questionnaires.

   TOTAL: _____
   NO. QUESTIONNAIRES: _____
   TOTAL RATING: _____
   (Teachers)

2. WHAT POSITIVE RESULTS FOR THE CHILD HAS THE HOME-BASED INSTRUCTION PROGRAM HAD, ACCORDING TO PARENTS? (Impacts: Parents)

```
|‒‒‒‒‒|‒‒‒‒‒|‒‒‒‒‒|‒‒‒‒‒|‒‒‒‒‒|‒‒‒‒‒|
1       1.5       2      2.5       3      3.5       4
```
Total Rating (Parents)

3. WHAT POSITIVE RESULTS FOR THE CHILD HAS THE HOME-BASED INSTRUCTION PROGRAM HAD, ACCORDING TO TEACHERS? (Impacts: Teachers)

```
|‒‒‒‒‒|‒‒‒‒‒|‒‒‒‒‒|‒‒‒‒‒|‒‒‒‒‒|‒‒‒‒‒|
1       1.5       2      2.5       3      3.5       4
```
Total Rating (Teachers)

# PARENT QUESTIONNAIRE:
# HOME-BASED INSTRUCTION SECTION

_____ I have used hints, ideas or materials provided by the school to help my child learn at home. (Answer questions below.)

_____ I have not used hints, ideas or materials provided by the school to help my child learn at home. (Please go on to next page.)

HOW DO YOU FEEL ABOUT THE STATEMENTS BELOW?
(Circle your choice.)

| | Strongly Agree | Agree | Disagree | Strongly Disagree |
|---|---|---|---|---|
| Helping my child learn at home has: | | | | |
| 1. Improved her/his attitude toward learning. | 4 | 3 | 2 | 1 |
| 2. Increased her/his attendance at school. | 4 | 3 | 2 | 1 |
| 3. Made her/him more comfortable with classwork. | 4 | 3 | 2 | 1 |
| 4. Made her/him more comfortable with homework. | 4 | 3 | 2 | 1 |
| 5. Helped her/him learn more. | 4 | 3 | 2 | 1 |

Total Ratings: _____ No. Items: ___5___ Average Rating: _____

# TEACHER QUESTIONNAIRE:
# HOME-BASED INSTRUCTION SECTION

_____ I have, or the school has, provided hints, ideas or materials for parents to use with their children at home. (Answer questions below.)

_____ I have not, and the school has not, provided hints, ideas or materials for parents to use with their children at home. (Please go to the next page.)

---

HOW DO YOU FEEL ABOUT THE STATEMENTS BELOW?
(Circle your choice.)

| | Strongly Agree | Agree | Disagree | Strongly Disagree |
|---|---|---|---|---|
| Parents' assistance to their children at home has: | | | | |
| 1. Improved students' attitudes toward learning. | 4 | 3 | 2 | 1 |
| 2. Increased students' attendance. | 4 | 3 | 2 | 1 |
| 3. Made students more comfortable with classwork. | 4 | 3 | 2 | 1 |
| 4. Made students more comfortable with homework. | 4 | 3 | 2 | 1 |
| 5. Helped students learn more. | 4 | 3 | 2 | 1 |

---

Total Ratings:_____ No. Items:____5____ Average Rating:_____

# VITAL INGREDIENTS CHECKLIST

| VITAL INGREDIENT | ✓ | ACTION STEPS | PAGE NO. |
|---|---|---|---|
| PROVIDE COORDINATION FOR ACTIVITIES | | Assign a person(s) at the district or school level to be responsible for:<br>(a) organizing training workshops;<br>(b) recruiting parents for workshops and home assignments;<br>(c) compiling lists of activities and materials for home use;<br>(d) following-up on specific assignments;<br>(e) providing necessary support services and supplies. | 11<br>50* |
| | | (Space for Local Action Steps) | |
| ASSESS NEEDS AND RESOURCES | | Assess (either formally or informally) student needs for home-based instruction. | 11<br>51* |
| | | Determine resources that can be used at home. | |
| | | Develop home-based instruction program based on student needs and resources available. | |
| | | (Space for Local Action Steps) | |
| SPECIFY AND COMMUNICATE PARENT ROLES | | Prepare a written statement that defines the parents' role as teachers of their own children at home. | 13<br>52* |
| | | Communicate parent roles to parents through media, pamphlets, handbooks, meetings, etc. | 14<br>53* |
| | | (Space for Local Action Steps) | |
| RECRUIT PARENT HOME – TEACHERS | | Use a variety of methods to inform parents of home-based instruction activities (for example, advertisements, meetings, events, workshops, personal contacts). | 14<br>54* |
| | | For certain programs, select and assign parents who are appropriate to participate in related activities (for example, remedial math home tutoring). | 15<br>54* |
| | | (Space for Local Action Steps) | |
| TRAIN PARENTS | | Provide a variety of training activities for parents that:<br>(a) demonstrate how to make and use materials;<br>(b) present a broad range of ideas on how to help children;<br>(c) provide resources for trainees to use;<br>(d) emphasize the importance of communication between parents and teachers. | 15<br>55* |

\* Handbook reference for "What Works: Successful Practices" relating to action steps.

# VITAL INGREDIENTS CHECKLIST

| VITAL INGREDIENT | √ | ACTION STEPS | PAGE NO. |
|---|---|---|---|
| TRAIN PARENTS (Continued) | | (Space for Local Action Steps) | |
| ESTABLISH COMMUNICATION CHANNELS | | Provide a variety of opportunities for teachers and parents to exchange ideas about home-teaching activities. | 16 |
| | | Give parents opportunities to express their feelings about participating in the home-based instruction program. | 16 57* |
| | | (Space for Local Action Steps) | |
| SUPPORT ONGOING ACTIVITIES | | Offer parents material services or supplies (such as child care or transportation) that will make it easier for them to attend workshops and conferences. | 18 57* |
| | | Recognize and reward the efforts of parents who participate in home-teaching activities. | |
| | | Establish procedures to monitor home activities that are directly related to particular skills being taught in class. | 18 58* |
| | | Determine ways to evaluate the overall home-teaching program for its strengths and weaknesses so that changes can be made. | |
| | | (Space for Local Action Steps) | |

* Handbook reference for "What Works: Successful Practices" relating to action steps.

# PARENTAL INVOLVEMENT PLANNING FORM

| | GOALS (PROFILE) | OBJECTIVES (VITAL INGREDIENTS/ ACTION STEPS) | TASKS | TARGET COMPLETION DATES |
|---|---|---|---|---|
| 3 MO | | | | |
| 6 MO | | | | |
| 9 MO | | | | |
| 1 YR | | | | |

# Profile Worksheet: Involving Parents in Instruction at School

The handbook presents five criteria for judging your success at getting parents involved in instruction at school:

1. *Parent aides are present in most classrooms.* A successful parent-aide program must include more than one or two parents. Since an overall goal is to help as many children as possible and get as many parents participating as possible, you should try to have parents involved in all classrooms. This won't always be possible, of course, but it is an ideal to work toward.

2. *Parent aides instruct students.* Aides may be assigned many duties both inside and outside the classroom. However, to maximize the benefits listed in the Handbook, aides should participate in the actual instruction of students in the classroom.

3. *Aides collaborate regularly with teachers about classroom activities.* Parents bring something special to the classroom: fluency in a language, familiarity with children of different cultures and ability to explain ideas in a particularly effective manner. They can be valuable resources in determining what is taught to whom, in what manner and at what pace. Parent aides need to feel that they are part of the instructional process. Teachers, in turn, can benefit from discussing their plans with someone who is familiar with the classroom setting. Therefore, parent aides and teachers should collaborate regularly to determine appropriate instructional strategies.

4. *The parent-aide program has continuity.* Although it is possible for many parents to serve as aides for brief periods of time, the quality of involvement is improved with long-term participation. Students and teachers need to know whom they can expect to work with at any given time. Parents need to see the results of their efforts to assist students and teachers. Thus, two or three parents who work at prescribed times in each classroom are preferable to many parents who periodically come and go.

5. *The parent-aide program has impact.* Parent aides should bring about benefits for the school. Students' achievement, attendance and attitude toward school should improve, as should teachers' attitudes. Parents' ability to help their own children should increase. Some effects may appear quickly, others more gradually. But in any case, successful parental involvement as instructional aides will have identifiable positive outcomes.

## Judging the Status of Your Parent-Aide Program

The questions that follow are based on the five criteria for success repeated above. Answer them here and then transfer your answers to the corresponding scale on the profile.

1. WHAT PERCENTAGE OF CLASSROOMS HAVE AT LEAST ONE PARENT WORKING AS A PAID OR VOLUNTEER AIDE? (% Classrooms)

2. WHAT PERCENTAGE OF TIME DOES THE AVERAGE PARENT AIDE SPEND ON INSTRUCTIONAL ACTIVITIES? (% Time on Instruction)

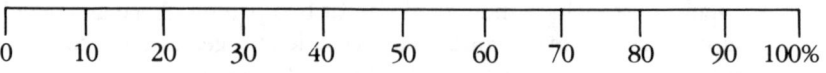

3. WHAT PERCENTAGE OF PARENT AIDES COLLABORATE WITH CLASSROOM TEACHERS IN PLANNING INSTRUCTIONAL STRATEGIES FOR CHILDREN? (% Planning Instruction)

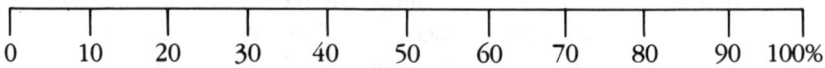

4. WHAT PERCENTAGE OF PARENT AIDES WORK IN A CLASSROOM AT LEAST ONCE A WEEK? (% Regular)

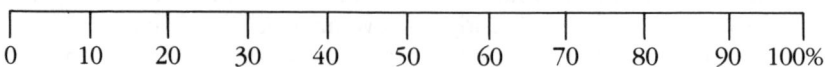

To complete the next two items, use the results from the school instructional aides section of the Parent and Teacher Questionnaires, following these steps:

1. Compute the AVERAGE RATING for *each* questionnaire.

   Add all the ratings on a questionnaire. Write the total at the bottom. Divide the total you just got by the number of items. Write that number—the average rating—at the bottom.

2. Compute the TOTAL RATINGS for *all* questionnaires.

   (a) Add all Parent Questionnaire average ratings.
   (b) Count the number of Parent Questionnaires.
   (c) Divide the total by the number of questionnaires.

TOTAL: _____

NO. QUESTIONNAIRES: _____

TOTAL RATING: _____

(Parents)

(a) Add all Teacher Questionnaire average ratings.
(b) Count the number of Teacher Questionnaires.
(c) Divide the total by the number of questionnaires.

TOTAL: _____

NO. QUESTIONNAIRES: _____

TOTAL RATING: _____

(Teachers)

5. WHAT IMPACTS HAS THE PARENT-AIDE PROGRAM HAD, ACCORDING TO PARENTS? (Impacts: Parents)

```
1        1.5        2        2.5        3        3.5        4
```
Total Rating (Parents)

6. WHAT IMPACTS HAS THE PARENT-AIDE PROGRAM HAD, ACCORDING TO TEACHERS? (Impacts: Teachers)

```
1        1.5        2        2.5        3        3.5        4
```
Total Rating (Teachers)

# PARENT QUESTIONNAIRE:
# SCHOOL INSTRUCTIONAL AIDES SECTION

———— I have worked in the classroom:
as a paid aide————; as a volunteer————————.
(Answer the questions below.)

———— I have not worked in the classroom as a paid aide or volunteer.
(Please go on to the next page.)

---

### HOW DO YOU FEEL ABOUT THE STATEMENTS BELOW?
(Circle your choice.)

| | Strongly Agree | Agree | Disagree | Strongly Disagree |
|---|---|---|---|---|
| 1. Working as an instructional aide has made me more knowledgeable about the school's educational program. | 4 | 3 | 2 | 1 |
| 2. Working as an instructional aide has helped me grow as an individual. | 4 | 3 | 2 | 1 |
| 3. My suggestions about instructional activities have led to some changes in instruction in the classroom or school. | 4 | 3 | 2 | 1 |
| Parent participation as instructional aides has: | | | | |
| 4. Tended to improve students' attitudes toward school; | 4 | 3 | 2 | 1 |
| 5. Helped students learn; | 4 | 3 | 2 | 1 |
| 6. Helped teachers in their teaching. | 4 | 3 | 2 | 1 |

---

Total Ratings: ————  No. Items: ——6——  Average Rating: ————

# TEACHER QUESTIONNAIRE:
# SCHOOL INSTRUCTIONAL AIDES SECTION

———— I have had parents working in my classroom:
as paid aides————; as volunteers ————————.
(Answer the questions below.)

———— I have not had parents working in my classroom as paid aides
or volunteers. (Please go on to the next page.)

HOW DO YOU FEEL ABOUT THE STATEMENTS BELOW?
(Circle your choice.)

| Parent participation as instructional aides has: | Strongly Agree | Agree | Disagree | Strongly Disagree |
|---|---|---|---|---|
| 1. Helped me to be more responsive to the individual needs of students. | 4 | 3 | 2 | 1 |
| 2. Helped me achieve my instructional goals. | 4 | 3 | 2 | 1 |
| 3. Tended to improve students' attitudes toward school. | 4 | 3 | 2 | 1 |
| 4. Helped students to learn. | 4 | 3 | 2 | 1 |
| 5. Improved the general educational climate within the school. | 4 | 3 | 2 | 1 |
| 6. Helped parents become more knowledgeable about the school's educational program. | 4 | 3 | 2 | 1 |
| 7. Led to some changes in instruction as a result of parent aides' suggestions. | 4 | 3 | 2 | 1 |

Total Ratings: ———— No. Items: ——7—— Average Rating: ————

# VITAL INGREDIENTS CHECKLIST

| VITAL INGREDIENT | √ | ACTION STEP | PAGE NO. |
|---|---|---|---|
| PROVIDE COORDINATION FOR ACTIVITIES | | Assign a person(s) at the district or school level to be responsible for:<br>(a) recruiting parent aides;<br>(b) matching parents' talents and availability with teachers' needs;<br>(c) providing necessary support services and supplies. | 11<br>64* |
| | | (Space for Local Action Steps) | |
| ASSESS NEEDS AND RESOURCES | | Assess (either formally or informally) teachers' needs for instructional assistance. | 11<br>65* |
| | | Assess (either formally or informally) parents' interests, skills and availability. | 11<br>65* |
| | | Use the findings from both assessments to organize the parent-aide program. | 11<br>66* |
| | | (Space for Local Action Steps) | |
| SPECIFY AND COMMUNICATE PARENT ROLES | | Prepare a written statement that defines specific roles, tasks and instructional duties for parent aides. | 13<br>67* |
| | | Involve parents, teachers and administrators in defining aides' roles. | 13 |
| | | Communicate the agreed-upon role to parents and teachers through pamphlets, handbooks, conferences, etc. | 14<br>67* |
| | | Make certain that the role statement is agreed upon by interested parents, staff and administrators. | 13<br>67* |
| | | Have individual teachers and parent aides meet to agree upon the aides' specific role in each classroom. | 66*<br>68* |
| | | If the program includes both paid and volunteer parent aides, differentiate the duties and responsibilities of each so that it is clear why some are paid and others are not. | 68* |
| | | (Space for Local Action Steps) | |

* Handbook references for "What Works: Successful Practices" relating to action steps.

# VITAL INGREDIENTS CHECKLIST

| VITAL INGREDIENT | √ | ACTION STEPS | PAGE NO. |
|---|---|---|---|
| RECRUIT, SELECT AND ASSIGN PARENT AIDES | | Provide a variety of opportunities for parents with diverse interests, skills and availability to participate in the school. | 14 68* |
| | | Use a variety of methods to inform parents of opportunities in the school (for example, principal and staff recommendations, telephone contacts, notices sent home, local advertising, etc.) | 14 70* |
| | | Develop ways for selecting and assigning parents to particular classrooms for particular duties. | 15 70* |
| | | (Space for Local Action Steps) | |
| TRAIN PARENTS AND STAFF | | Provide preservice and inservice training for parent aides on: (a) aides' overall responsibilities in the classroom; (b) school rules and procedures; (c) specific teaching techniques; (d) classroom management practices. | 71* |
| | | Provide preservice and inservice training for teachers on: (a) how to determine appropriate activities for aides; (b) how to plan an aide's time in the classroom; (c) how to monitor aide's work; (d) how to communicate effectively with aides. | 71* |
| | | Schedule at least some training sessions that allow parents and staff to work together. | 16 |
| | | Survey parents and teachers to schedule training at times that are convenient to everyone. | 72* |
| | | Plan training on the basis of formal or informal assessments of teacher and parent needs. | 15 |
| | | Evaluate the training and use these evaluations to plan future training. | 16 |
| | | (Space for Local Action Steps) | |

* Handbook reference for "What Works: Successful Practices" relating to action steps.

# VITAL INGREDIENTS CHECKLIST

| VITAL INGREDIENT | ✓ | ACTION STEPS | PAGE NO. |
|---|---|---|---|
| ESTABLISH COMMUNI-CATION CHANNELS | | Develop communication channels between the district/school and aides to keep aides informed of district policies and events, inservice training opportunities and job openings. | 17 74* |
| | | Actively promote regular meetings and other forms of communication between teachers and aides. | 17 74* |
| | | Actively promote regular meetings and other forms of communication among aides. | 17 74* |
| | | (Space for Local Action Steps) | |
| SUPPORT ONGOING ACTIVITIES | | Offer parents material services or supplies (such as transportation reimbursements or babysitting) that will make it easier for them to work as aides. | 18 75* |
| | | Recognize and reward the instructional contributions of individual parent aides. | 18 76* |
| | | Establish procedures for carefully monitoring the parent-aide program, in order to demonstrate its importance and to tell whether assignments for aides need to be revised, whether more or fewer aides are needed, and whether those aides and teachers already in the program think it worthwhile. | 18 76* |
| | | (Space for Local Action Steps) | |

* Handbook references for "What Works: Successful Practices" relating to action steps.

# PARENTAL INVOLVEMENT PLANNING FORM

| | GOALS (PROFILE) | OBJECTIVES (VITAL INGREDIENTS/ ACTION STEPS) | TASKS | TARGET COMPLETION DATES |
|---|---|---|---|---|
| **3 MO** | | | | |
| **6 MO** | | | | |
| **9 MO** | | | | |
| **1 YR** | | | | |

# Profile Worksheet: Involving Parents in Advisory Groups

The handbook presents three criteria for judging the successful involvement of your advisory group in the school:

1. *The parent advisory group gets involved in significant school-related areas.* A parent advisory group ought to participate in making important decisions. Our study showed that the most active groups helped make decisions about: (1) curriculum, or what instructional services are offered to students; (2) the budget, or how funds are allocated; (3) personnel, or who provides educational services to students; and (4) parent activities, or how parents are to participate in schools.

2. *This involvement occurs regularly.* The parent advisory group contributes regularly to decisions on educational matters. For example, a one-time screening of paid-aide applications is not considered successful involvement. A group should be meeting periodically to discuss issues and to make recommendations to decision makers.

3. *This involvement has impact.* Parent advisory group recommendations are listened to and, on occasion, lead to action. In other words, there should be some evidence that the group's advice has actually influenced decisions made by district or school staff.

## Judging the Status of Your Parent Advisory Group

The questions that follow are based on these three criteria and ask you to judge the role that your advisory group plays in each of the four decision areas listed in the first criterion.

When answering each question, think about the decisions that have been made in the school or district over the past year in an area. Then decide how you would describe your advisory group's role in *most of* those decisions. Use these definitions to help decide where you would place your advisory group on a continuum from "no involvement" to "major involvement" in school or district decisions.

| | |
|---|---|
| No Involvement | The advisory group was not even informed about activities in a given area and was never asked to advise on any decisions that were made in that area. |
| Informed Only | The advisory group was kept informed about activities in the area, but was not asked for any advice. |

| Minor Role | The advisory group was "asked" for advice about decisions, but for the most part it went along with staff recommendations with little discussion or advice being offered. |
| Major Role | The advisory group gave advice that was regularly heeded by school or district decision makers. The group was an important part of the overall decision process in the area. |

1. WHAT ROLE DOES YOUR ADVISORY GROUP PLAY IN DECISIONS ABOUT CURRICULUM OR INSTRUCTIONAL SERVICES TO BE OFFERED TO STUDENTS? (Role: Curriculum)

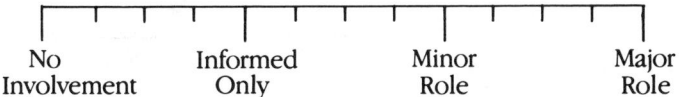

| No Involvement | Informed Only | Minor Role | Major Role |

2. WHAT ROLE DOES YOUR ADVISORY GROUP PLAY IN DECISIONS ABOUT THE BUDGET OR HOW MONEY WILL BE SPENT (OTHER THAN ITS OWN BUDGET)? (Role: Budget)

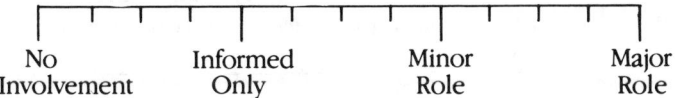

| No Involvement | Informed Only | Minor Role | Major Role |

3. WHAT ROLE DOES YOUR ADVISORY GROUP PLAY IN DECISIONS ABOUT PERSONNEL? (Role: Personnel)

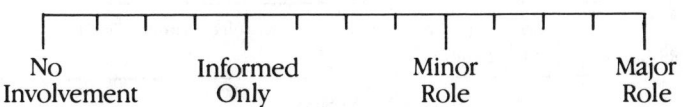

| No Involvement | Informed Only | Minor Role | Major Role |

4. WHAT ROLE DOES YOUR ADVISORY GROUP PLAY IN DECISIONS ABOUT PARENT ACTIVITIES? (Role: Parent Activities)

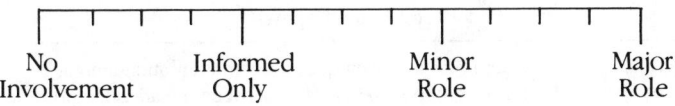

| No Involvement | Informed Only | Minor Role | Major Role |

# VITAL INGREDIENTS CHECKLIST

| VITAL INGREDIENT | ✓ | ACTION STEPS | PAGE NO. |
|---|---|---|---|
| PROVIDE COORDINATION FOR ACTIVITIES | | Give someone authority and responsibility for seeing that:<br>(a) parent members are recruited or elected;<br>(b) the advisory group receives training;<br>(c) meeting logistics are satisfied;<br>(d) the advisory group receives needed support. | 11<br>81* |
| | | (Space for Local Action Steps) | |
| ASSESS NEEDS AND RESOURCES | | Conduct an assessment to determine decision areas for advisory group involvement. | 5<br>82* |
| | | Survey parent members to identify related skills and experience. | 5<br>82* |
| | | (Space for Local Action Steps) | |
| SPECIFY AND COMMUNICATE ADVISORY GROUP ROLES | | Involve parents and staff in defining roles for the advisory group. | 13<br>84* |
| | | Inform parents and staff of the roles to be played by the advisory group. | 14<br>84* |
| | | (Space for Local Action Steps) | |
| RECRUIT AND SELECT PARENT MEMBERS | | Use a variety of techniques to interest parents in serving on the advisory group. | 14<br>85* |
| | | Apply a process systematically to select parents for the advisory group. | 15<br>86* |
| | | (Space for Local Action Steps) | |
| TRAIN PARENTS AND STAFF | | Provide training to the advisory group on the subject matter for decisions and on group processes. | 15<br>88* |
| | | (Space for Local Action Steps) | |
| ESTABLISH COMMUNI- CATION CHANNELS | | Put into practice techniques for communication among advisory group members, and between the advisory group and the school. | 17<br>89* |
| | | (Space for Local Action Steps) | |

* Handbook reference for "What Works: Successful Practices" relating to the Action Steps.

# VITAL INGREDIENTS CHECKLIST

| VITAL INGREDIENT | √ | ACTION STEPS | PAGE NO. |
|---|---|---|---|
| SUPPORT ONGOING ACTIVITIES | | Provide services and supplies that the advisory group needs to function effectively. | 18 91* |
| | | Monitor the advisory group to verify that it is succeeding in meeting its objectives. | 18 92* |
| | | (Space for Local Action Steps) | |

\* Handbook reference for "What Works: Successful Practices" relating to the action steps.

# PARENTAL INVOLVEMENT PLANNING FORM

| | GOALS (PROFILE) | OBJECTIVES (VITAL INGREDIENTS/ ACTION STEPS) | TASKS | TARGET COMPLETION DATES |
|---|---|---|---|---|
| 3 MO | | | | |
| 6 MO | | | | |
| 9 MO | | | | |
| 1 YR | | | | |

# PART III

*Resource Guide*

# Resource Guide

*This part of the handbook is intended to help you get as much information and assistance as possible as you fashion meaningful parental involvement in your district. The resources discussed fall into three major categories: reading materials, forms/documents and people. The first section of the Resource Guide presents reading materials and forms/documents that have been used with success in organizing parental involvement activities. The second section describes a set of procedures for locating people who can provide services in the areas of training and technical assistance. Each section is preceded by its own brief introduction.*

# Bibliography/ Resource Index

This section contains a bibliography and resource index of pertinent books and materials that can be used to help school administrators develop parent programs. This section also contains sample forms that we thought would be useful, for example, when organizing a new volunteer program or conducting an advisory group survey. We feel these materials can contribute to coordinating successful practices in the area of parental involvement.

The reference materials have been divided into major categories. The bibliography sources are listed first, followed by the resource materials and sample forms. Any bibliographic entry marked with an asterisk has the same publisher as the previous entry.

— HOME-SCHOOL RELATIONSHIPS (material that deals with developing positive interpersonal relations between parents and school personnel)

— SCHOOL SUPPORT (resource material that offers ways for schools to obtain support from parents for their operations, such as fund-raising)

— PARENT EDUCATION (information concerning educational programs or books that can teach parents about parent-child relations, parenting skills, health and nutrition, etc.)

— HOME-BASED INSTRUCTION (ideas that parents can use to help their children learn at home)

— INSTRUCTION AT SCHOOL (materials for aides and volunteers who work with children in the classroom)

— ADVISORY GROUPS (materials related to the organization of parent advisory groups, suggested advisory group activities and information concerning involvement of parents)

— SUPPLEMENTARY MATERIAL FOR STAFF (additional information pertaining to parent involvement that may be of interest to school and district staff)

# HOME-SCHOOL RELATIONSHIPS BIBLIOGRAPHY

TITLE: *School-Community Interaction*

AUTHOR: Richard W. Saxe

PUBLISHER: McCutchan Publishing Corporation
Berkeley, CA: 1975

MAJOR IDEAS: The purpose of this book is to describe changes in school-community interaction and to suggest appropriate responses by educators in general, and administrators in particular. This is done by addressing the problems of school-community interaction. The book may be used by a group interested in school-community interaction or by staff who wish to supplement or validate the central ideas presented in the individual chapters by performing some of the suggested activities at the ends of the chapters. The suggested activities are listed as ways of testing the author's concepts against the real, specific school-community interaction in the several areas available for study by readers. Some topics covered in the book include: Community Relations: Semantics, p. 5; School District Organization, Bureaucracy and Schools, p. 17; Educators' Opinions of Community Relations, p. 33; Determining Community Resources, p. 141; Two-Way Communication, p. 163; On Citizen Participation, p. 229. Appropriate for staff. (265 pp.)

TITLE:      *Planning and Implementing Parent/Community Involvement into the Instructional Delivery System: Proceedings from a Parent/Community Involvement Conference*

AUTHOR:     Charles Barletta, Robert Boger, Lawrence Lezotte and Beth Hull, Editors

PUBLISHER:  The Midwest Teacher Corps Network
East Lansing, MI: 1978

MAJOR IDEAS: This book contains documentation of the proceedings from a Parent/Community Involvement Conference sponsored by the Midwest Teacher Corps Network of Michigan State University which brought together six of the Parent/Community Models that are recognized as excellent examples of home/school cooperation. These models were designed to help both teachers and parents to work more effectively with the child. Contents include: Systematic Use of Human Resources: Structured Tutoring, p. 24; Preparing Educators for Parent Involvement, p. 44; Parents are Teachers Too, p. 52; Community Involvement Activities: Research into Action, p. 12. Appropriate for staff and parents. (104 pp., Bibliography included.)

TITLE:      *Building Effective Home-School Relationships*

AUTHOR:     Ira J. Gordon and William F. Breivogel, Editors

PUBLISHER:  Allyn and Bacon, Inc.
Boston, MA: 1976

MAJOR IDEAS: The aim of this book is to offer practical suggestions in which "social people" and parents can work together for the enhancement of the learning of children. Discussions focus on: Toward a Home-School Partnership Program, p. 1; Training for Home Visitations, p. 53; Home Learning Activities for Children, p. 130; Designing an Evaluation for Home-School Programs, p. 149. Appropriate for staff and parents. (239 pp.; Bibliography included.)

| | |
|---|---|
| TITLE: | *Teachers and Parents: A Guide to Instruction and Cooperation* |
| AUTHOR: | Robert B. Rutherford, Jr. and Eugene Edgar |
| PUBLISHER: | Allyn and Bacon, Inc.<br>Boston, MA: 1979 |
| MAJOR IDEAS: | The book describes systematic procedures that teachers can follow when dealing with those student problems best addressed through cooperative efforts with parents. It provides a rationale for teacher-parent cooperative endeavors and offers specific techniques for interacting with parents in various situations—all designed to enhance the effectiveness of teachers and parents in working with each other and in dealing with the children for whom they share responsibility. Section discussions include: Exchange of Information, p. 3; Teacher-Parent Cooperation, p. 19; Interpersonal Communication Skills, p. 77. Appropriate for staff. (254 pp.) |

| | |
|---|---|
| TITLE: | *School, Family and Neighborhood: The Theory and Practice of School-Community Relations* |
| AUTHOR: | Eugene Litwak and Henry J. Meyer |
| PUBLISHER: | Columbia University Press<br>New York, NY: 1974 |
| MAJOR IDEAS: | The book offers guidelines to practitioners concerned with local school-community relations of educational institutions. Practical suggestions are offered, sometimes in prescriptive language as proposals for action rather than as rules. The two sections of the book include: Part One, School-Community Relations: Theoretical Framework; and Part Two, Mechanisms for Linking School and Community. Appropriate for staff. (300 pp.) |

| | |
|---|---|
| TITLE: | *101 Pupil/Parent/Teacher Situations and How to Handle Them* |
| AUTHOR: | P. Susan Mamchak and Steven R. Mamchak |

| | |
|---|---|
| PUBLISHER: | Parker Publishing Company, Inc.<br>West Nyack, NY: 1980 |
| MAJOR IDEAS: | This book contains 101 of the most challenging situations faced by teachers in their dealings with students, parents and even other teachers. In each case a corrective action is given, and in many cases, more than one. They are courses of action that are educationally sound, ultimately effective and specifically designed to prevent recurrence in the future. Subject topics include: Communicating with the Non-Involved Parent, p. 70; Methods of Dealing with the Hostile Parent, p. 77; Involving Parents in Disciplinary Decisions, p. 96; Getting Parents to Participate in Academic Actions, p. 104. Appropriate for staff. (225 pp.) |
| TITLE: | *Home/School/Community Interaction: What We Know and Why We Don't Know More* |
| AUTHOR: | Cynthia Wallat and Richard Goldman |
| PUBLISHER: | Charles E. Merrill Publishing Co.<br>Columbus, OH: 1979 |
| MAJOR IDEAS: | This book is intended as a guide, a manual of reference or a set of working tools for parents, educators and students who intend to contribute their services to educational concerns. It provides a summation of what the authors know about the development of school/community communication and a guide to future ventures which recognize the school's capacity for positive contributions to society. The book contains descriptions of successful home/school programs, parent education programs, advice articles and references to inexpensive information sources. These may serve as the focus of class or group discussions. Data from research studies are also included to convince the reader of the importance of school-community communication. Topics of discussion include: Parents as Educators, p.129; Parents as Contributors to Decision Making, p. 129. Appropriate for staff. (232 pp.; Bibliography included.) |

| TITLE: | *Elementary Teachers Guide to Working with Parents* |
|---|---|
| AUTHOR: | Helen Heffernan and Vivian Edmiston Todd |
| PUBLISHER: | Parker Publishing Company, Inc.<br>West Nyack, NY: 1969 |
| MAJOR IDEAS: | This book presents various techniques that make for good rapport between school and parents. Topics include: Developing the Basis for a Conference, p. 19; Building an Effective Rapport with Parents, p. 35; Securing Parental Involvement, p. 133; Developing Program Innovations, p. 155; Preparing School Personnel for Parent Conferences, p. 185. Appropriate for staff. (210 pp.) |

| TITLE: | *Between Parent and School* |
|---|---|
| AUTHOR: | Murray M. Kappelman, M.D. and Paul R. Ackerman, Ph.D. |
| PUBLISHER: | The Dial Press/James Wade<br>New York, NY: 1977 |
| MAJOR IDEAS: | The major focus of this book is to state that parents often underestimate their impact upon the school system when ultimately change for the specific child has to occur at the local school level. Each child will be helped only when there is sufficient rapport and understanding between parent, teacher and school. This teamwork, geared toward creating a flexible school environment that can adjust to every child, should be the ultimate goal of parent, school and system. To enter this team, the parent must know what the other members do in their jobs, what their expectations and objectives are and how the team as a whole can best be utilized in the school setting. In addition, the book points out that a parent must understand his/her own child, the special problems and possible solutions, the alternate routes to maximum education and the options for the future. Part I, The Insiders, talks about the role and function of the school staff; Part II, Children, focuses on the special learning problems of the child; and Part III, Parent Power, presents ways in which parents can |

serve as advocates for their child's education needs. Appropriate for parents. (296 pp.; Resource list for parents included.)

TITLE: *Working Together: A Guide to Parent Involvement*

AUTHOR: Anthony J. Coletta, Ph.D.

PUBLISHER: Humanics Limited
Atlanta, GA: 1977

MAJOR IDEAS: The concepts presented throughout this book are aimed at renewing the sense of trust between home and school and creating a partnership based on clear communication and reciprocity. In the best sense of the term, this text envisions parents and teachers "working together" once more.

# HOME-SCHOOL RELATIONSHIPS
# RESOURCE MATERIALS

TITLE: *Parents—Your Involvement Can Help Your Child*

PUBLISHER: Moreno Educational Company
7050 Belle Glade Lane
San Diego, CA 92119

MAJOR IDEAS: The author shows the value of parental involvement in the child's school. He gives helpful hints on how parents can get to know school personnel and vice versa. This illustrated 32-page booklet gives step-by-step methods for helping parents become interested and involved in school activities. Written in Spanish and English.

TITLE: *The Flexible Learning System, "Communicating and Working with Parents"*

AUTHOR: Margaret Robinson

PUBLISHER: Far West Laboratory
San Francisco, CA

COMMENTS: Available through ERIC #ED 129 456.

TITLE:   *Program Handbook:*
         *Parent-School-Community Involvement*
         *and Parent Education*

PUBLISHER:   Southwest Educational Development Lab and
             Texas Education Agency
             Austin, TX

MAJOR IDEAS:   This handbook contains a variety of suggestions on
               how to pull together the parents, the school and the
               community. It gives many specific examples of
               activities.

TITLE:   *Single Parents and the Public Schools: How the*
         *Partnership Works*

PUBLISHER:   National Committee for Citizens in Education
             Wilde Lake Village Green, Suite 410
             Columbia, MD 21044

MAJOR IDEAS:   The 77-page paper discusses programs and policies
               that schools have that are responsive to single-parent
               families. Included are suggestions for parents and
               suggestions for schools. ($3.25)

TITLE:   *Working with Parents (A Guide for Classroom*
         *Teachers and Other Educators)*

PUBLISHER:   National School Public Relations Association
             Washington, DC

MAJOR IDEAS:   This brochure has practical suggestions for teachers
               on how to contact parents and how to talk to parents
               about a variety of topics. Very helpful to elementary
               and secondary teachers, and gives ideas to the parent
               coordinator for working more effectively with
               parents.

TITLE:   *Working With the Bilingual Community*

PUBLISHER:   National Clearinghouse for Bilingual Education
             1300 Wilson Blvd., Suite B2-11
             Rosslyn, VA 22209

MAJOR IDEAS: An anthology of papers discussing the importance of parent and community involvement in bilingual education programs. (90 pp. $4.50)

TITLE: *NSBA Bibliography on Multicultural Education* *

AUTHOR: Jack Levy

MAJOR IDEAS: Lists books, films and television programs designed to help educators promote intercultural tolerance. (49 pp. $4.90)

# SCHOOL-SUPPORT BIBLIOGRAPHY

TITLE: *Organizing School Volunteer Programs*

AUTHOR: Barbara Carter and Gloria Dapper

PUBLISHER: Citation Press
New York, NY: 1974

MAJOR IDEAS: Outlines how to develop an efficient and innovative volunteer program in the schools. Discusses organizational recruitment and screening of volunteers, providing orientation and training, serving as liaison between the schools and the volunteers, initiating new programs and services, providing in-service training workshops, searching for funding and coordinating efforts with other organizations in the community. Appropriate for staff. (162 pp.)

TITLE: *Parent Volunteer Programs in Early Childhood Education: A Practical Guide*

AUTHOR: Henry C. Brook, III

PUBLISHER: Linnet Books
Hamden, CT: 1976

MAJOR IDEAS: This is a practical resource book for parents, teachers, librarians and administrators now involved, or considering becoming involved, in a parent volunteer program. Includes sections discussing: Orientation Information for Parent Volunteers, p. 56; Attendance Records, p. 59; Volunteer Information, p. 60; Library Publications, p. 61; Parent Coordinator Job Description, p. 63; and other staff job descriptions (i.e., secretarial, grounds supervisor, clerk), pp. 68-72; Volunteer Self-Education, p. 79; Supervisor Evaluation of the Volunteer, p. 92. Book provides excellent models of questionnaires, evaluation forms, parent award designs, cover letters to parents, volunteer record of attendance, job descriptions, program library publications list, etc. Appropriate for staff. (114 pp.; Bibliography included.)

# SCHOOL-SUPPORT RESOURCE MATERIAL

| | |
|---|---|
| TITLE: | *Fund-Raising by Parent/Citizen Groups* |
| PUBLISHER: | National Committee for Citizens in Education<br>Wilde Lake Village Green, Suite 410<br>Columbia, MD 21044 |
| MAJOR IDEAS: | A step-by-step guide to fund-raising activities. Takes parents and citizens through the basics, from identifying sources of support to the development of a fund-raising plan. Tells how to handle follow-up and cultivate donors; includes sample proposals, suggestions on how to form a tax-exempt organization, tips on reporting back to donors. (52 pp. $2.50) |

| | |
|---|---|
| TITLE: | *Volunteers in Public Schools (VIPS) Handbook* |
| AUTHOR: | Houston Public Schools |
| PUBLISHER: | Volunteers in Public Schools<br>Houston, TX |
| MAJOR IDEAS: | This handbook summarizes the Houston volunteer program—its history, guidelines for volunteers and school staff members, guidelines for human relations. It also describes each volunteer project as well as procedures and policies. |

TITLE: *How To Organize a School Volunteer Program in Individual Schools, and Suggested Volunteer Aids*

PUBLISHER: Los Angeles City Unified School
District Volunteer and Tutorial Programs
Los Angeles, CA

MAJOR IDEAS: The booklet contains suggestions for organizing a program. Some of the sample forms might be very helpful.


TITLE: *Partners for the Eighties: Business and Education*

PUBLISHER: National School Volunteer Program, Inc.
300 North Washington Street
Alexandria, VA 22314

MAJOR IDEAS: This is a compendium of 24 outstanding models of local partnerships between the business community and the schools. Models include: adopt-a-school, mentor, community resource and internship programs. Order #P-4. ($5)


TITLE: *Partners for the Eighties: Handbook for Teachers*\*

MAJOR IDEAS: A 24-page handbook for teachers who work with school volunteers or who want to learn effective management techniques for school volunteer involvement. Order #P-5. ($2.75)


TITLE: *School Volunteer Programs: Everything You Need To Know to Start or Improve Your Program*\*

MAJOR IDEAS: This book includes tips for setting up a district-wide program, recruiting, orienting, training, working with teachers, maintaining volunteer morale and evaluating your program. Sample forms are included. Order #P-4. ($3)


TITLE: *School Volunteer Programs*\*

MAJOR IDEAS: (15 minutes, slide-tape presentation)
Shows how organized school volunteer programs tap the resources of the community to provide extra

help for teachers and students and how, in the process, volunteers become bridges to the community. Order #ST-400. (Rental — $15/month.)

TITLE:     *Toward a More Caring Society**

MAJOR IDEAS:     (12 minutes, slide-tape presentation)
A documentary of former First Lady Rosalynn Carter's visit to the school volunteer program of Springfield, MA. This presentation is excellent for recruiting and orientation of volunteers and for recognition events. Order #ST-500. (Rental — $15/month.)

TITLE:     *101 Activities for Building More Effective School-Community Involvement*

PUBLISHER:     The Home and School Institute, Inc.
1707 H Street, N.W.
Washington, DC 20006

MAJOR IDEAS:     This is a guide for parental involvement in the PTA and other community activities, focusing on interpersonal skills and locating available community resources. ($8)

TITLE:     *Reaching the Neighborhood Parent*

AUTHOR:     Anna W. M. Wolf, Adele B. Tunick

PUBLISHER:     National School Volunteer Program
(of the Public Education Association)
New York, NY

MAJOR IDEAS:     This brochure suggests ways to contact parents, attacks myths about minority group parents, discusses ways to talk to parents and describes successful parent groups in Detroit, Philadelphia, Cleveland and New York.

TITLE:            *Your Volunteer Program*

AUTHOR:           Mary T. Swanson

PUBLISHER:        Des Moines Area Community College
                  Des Moines, IA

MAJOR IDEAS:      This is a good handbook for a general volunteer
                  program. It is especially helpful in areas on
                  promoting volunteer programs and recruiting and
                  keeping volunteers. It also has a good bibliography
                  on many topics.

# Sample
# School-Support Forms

# SAMPLE PARENT INTEREST SURVEY *

Dear Mr. and Mrs. _____

I am asking for your help in order to enrich and enlarge your child's program at school.

Do you have a hobby to share? _____ If yes, specify. _____

_____

Do you have a talent you are willing to share (cooking, sewing, woodworking, music, art, dramatics, other)? _____

If yes, what? _____

Have you had experiences you are willing to share (travel, etc.)? _____ If yes, please specify. _____

Do you have an occupation or an association with a local business or industry of interest to children? _____ If yes, please specify. _____

Would you be interested in helping with any of the following? _____ If so, please check.

| | |
|---|---|
| _____ Telephoning | _____ Tutoring |
| _____ Cutting out pictures | _____ Bulletin boards |
| _____ Typing | _____ Library research |
| _____ Pasting | _____ Filing |

Do you have some ideas of ways you'd like to become more involved in such a school program? _____

What time would you be able to be with us? Please check.

| | |
|---|---|
| _____ Before school | _____ Afternoon |
| _____ Morning | _____ After school |
| _____ Noon | _____ Other |

Are there others in your family or neighborhood who would be interested in this program? _____ If yes, please specify. _____

_____
(Sign as desired)

---

*Elliot L. Richardson, Meeting Parents Halfway—A Guide for Schools. Washington: U.S. Office of Education, Department of Health, Education and Welfare, 1970, p. 16.

# SCHOOL VOLUNTEER APPLICATION

**Basic Information**

Name _____ Address _____

Phone _____

How many children in school? _____

Names                                  Teacher's Name(s)

_____ Grade ____ _____

_____ Grade ____ _____

_____ Grade ____ _____

_____ Grade ____ _____

Please note here any past experience you have had as a volunteer in schools or any other community activity. Note such things as activities, time spent, whether you worked alone or in a team situation.

**Volunteer Commitment**

Do you have any preference as to what you would like to do? (e.g., classroom work, clerical, library, etc.)

How many hours per week could you spend volunteering in school? ___

Would you be willing to undergo foundation training for volunteer work? (e.g., attend workshops, training meetings, etc.) _____

**Areas of Expertise**

Please note here any areas of expertise you may have. These may be professional skills, such as typing, clerical work, librarianship, health worker or any other skills you may have.

Other areas of help may be related to hobbies or pastime activities, such as weaving, pottery, reading, macrame, woodworking, needlepoint, painting, etc.

You also may have experience in some areas of enrichment such as playing a musical instrument, drama work, poetry appreciation, creative writing or singing. Please note these here if you would be willing to share them with children.

Please return this form to the Parent Coordinator when completed. Thank you for being interested in our Volunteer Program.

# APPEAL FOR SCHOOL VOLUNTEERS

Dear Parents,

On Tuesday, May 27, 1980, we will have a special day called Sixth Grade Day. This day is planned for sixth grade students and their parents. Following is a schedule of the day's activities:

| | |
|---|---|
| 9:15 - 10:15 | Spelling Bee |
| 10:15 - 11:30 | Academic Games |
| 11:45 - 1:30 | Lunch and Awards Ceremony |
| 1:45 - 3:10 | Talent Show and Fashion Show |

You are welcome to come to any or all of the activities.

We will have a special lunch prepared for the students by the cafeteria staff. We are asking that the parents send cakes or pies on Sixth Grade Day so the students will have a special dessert. Also, please send cakes or pies only.

There is a lot of work to be done in preparing for Sixth Grade Day. Therefore, we need a committee of parents to help. We will need parents to help decorate the cafeteria on Monday, May 26, and to serve desserts on Tuesday, May 27. Please help us if you can. We want this day to be a great success for your children. Since this is a special day, please ask your children to dress appropriately. It is very important that we know if you are coming to eat lunch with your child, so the cafeteria staff can prepare enough food. Please check the appropriate boxes below.

Sincerely,

. . . . . . . . . . . . . . . . . . . . . . . . . . . . . . . . . . . . . . . . . . . . . . . . . . . . .

☐   I will help decorate the cafeteria on Monday, May 26.

☐   I will help serve desserts on Tuesday, May 27.

☐   I plan to come and have lunch with my child. (Cost $1.15)

☐   I will send a dessert on Tuesday, May 27.   CAKE ☐   PIE ☐

_____
Parent's Signature

_____
Child's Name

_____
Homebase Teacher

# PARENT EDUCATION
# BIBLIOGRAPHY

TITLE:      *Parent Education*

AUTHOR:      Evelyn Pickarts and Jean Fargo

PUBLISHER:      Meredith Corporation
New York, NY: 1971

MAJOR IDEAS:      This book is addressed to people in the educational and mental health fields who deal in some way with the confusion parents feel about child-rearing, and who see the preventive task that confronts them. The book attempts to come to grips with the difficult problems facing those professions and agencies as they search for effective approaches. Topics of discussion include: Parents Are the Prime Teachers of Their Children, p. 5; The Learning-Valuing Focus: A Teachable Content for Parent Education Programs, p. 31; Adult Learning, p. 87; The Parent Educator: Selection, Preparation and Training, p. 117. Appropriate for staff. (311 pp.)

TITLE:      *The Family as Educator*

AUTHOR:      Hope Jensen Leichter, Editor

PUBLISHER:      Teachers College Press
Columbia University
New York, NY: 1974

MAJOR IDEAS:      The purpose of the book (a collection of essays) is to convey that education within the family is a fascinating subject in its own right and one that holds great promise as a field for systematic investigation. The idea for this book originated from a composium on "The Family as Educator" held at the May 1973 meeting of the National Academy of Education. Topics of discussion focus on: Perspectives on the Family as Educator, p. 1; Parental Goals: A Cross-Cultural View, p. 52; Grandparents as Educators, p. 66; Economic Aspects of the Family as Educator, p. 92. Appropriate for staff. (129 pp.)

| TITLE: | *Guidance of the Young Child* |
|---|---|
| AUTHOR: | Louise M. Langford and Helene Y. Rand |
| PUBLISHER: | John Wiley and Son, Inc.<br>New York, NY: 1975 |
| MAJOR IDEAS: | This book presents basic facts concerning child development and various points of view relative to child guidance in such a way that the student can formulate an individual and personal philosophy of guidance. Instead of a detailed account of human development and teaching theory, the book is intended as an introduction for students who will do further course work and research before they assume responsible positions in guiding groups of children. However, the information provided should be helpful to all adults who want to learn something about how children develop, and who want to recognize signs of progress toward the maturity of the child. Topics include: Types and Techniques of Guidance, p. 24; Physical and Motor Development, p. 42; Personality Development, p. 58; Social Development, p. 76; Language Development, p. 94; Learning, p. 114; Sleep and Rest, p. 144; Food for Children, p. 156; The Meaning and Value of Play, p. 184; Stories, Poems and Television, p. 218. Appropriate for staff and parents. (281 pp.) |

| TITLE: | *Prime-Time Parenting* |
|---|---|
| AUTHOR: | Kay Kuzma |
| PUBLISHER: | Rawson, Wade Publishers, Inc.<br>New York, NY: 1980 |
| MAJOR IDEAS: | This book is directed toward working parents who are striving to be prime-time parents—parents who are vitally interested in maintaining positive relationships with their children even though their work schedules permit less than a twenty-four-hour-a-day vigil. Contents include: Quality Time Together: The Key to Success, p. 3; Sharing the Child-Care Responsibility, p. 31; Working Parents and Their Problems, p. 60; Prime-Time Discipline: The Preventive Approach, p. 175; Solving Job and Family Conflicts, p. 228. Appropriate for parents. (305 pp.) |

| | |
|---|---|
| TITLE: | *The Learning Child* |
| AUTHOR: | Dorothy H. Cohen |
| PUBLISHER: | Pantheon Books<br>New York, NY: 1972 |
| MAJOR IDEAS: | This book discusses at length the styles of growth and learning that seem characteristic of large numbers of children who grew up under reasonably good home conditions. Three stages of the early school years are discussed. First, the five-year-olds and the contemporary confusion about beginning reading. Second are the six- and seven-year-olds and the need during the primary years for an intellectually stimulating life which the current three Rs curriculum does not by itself satisfy. And, third, is the period from eight to eleven, in which the first major identification with the values of the adult world creates serious questions as to how school and home learning can support moral growth and personal integrity. Contents include: Kindergarten and the Parent, p. 98; Intellectual Life in the Primary Grade, p. 144; Eight to Eleven: The Intermediate Years, p. 205; Parent and Child During the Intermediate Years, p. 297. Appropriate for staff and parents. (360 pp.) |

## PARENT EDUCATION
## RESOURCE MATERIALS

| | |
|---|---|
| TITLE: | *How to Listen to Your Child,* and<br>*How to Get Your Child to Listen to You* |
| AUTHOR: | Don E. Hamachek |
| PUBLISHER: | National Education Association<br>Order Department<br>The Academic Building<br>Saw Mill Road<br>West Haven, CT 06516 |
| MAJOR IDEAS: | Ideas are reinforced that parents have to listen to their children if good relations between them are to exist, and if they want their children to listen to |

them now and in the teen years. (Two cassette tapes, two filmstrips and guide, 10 minutes each. Also, a 14-page illustrated booklet.)

| | |
|---|---|
| TITLE: | *Parent/Teacher Game* |
| PUBLISHER: | Educational Planning and Product Development<br>7416 Twin Brook Circle<br>Chattanooga, TN 37421 |
| MAJOR IDEAS: | Bingo-type game for 6-24 players with calling cards and markers. Parents and teachers learn more about rearing and teaching children. The game calls attention to and reinforces parent/child and teacher/child relationships. The ideas that are presented can be discussed while the game is in progress. |

| | |
|---|---|
| TITLE: | *Enjoy Your Child* (series): Three illustrated paper-backs. (1) "Enjoy Your Child," (2) "Enjoy Your Child at Home," (3) "Enjoy Your Child at Home and School." Good for anyone interested in children.* |
| MAJOR IDEAS: | These booklets share several ideas: (1) be positive with children, (2) discipline should be firm but fair, (3) behavior is molded by example, etc. Good general reading for parents. Provides "how-to's" and "how-not-to's" when working with children. |

| | |
|---|---|
| TITLE: | *Setting Limits and Rules for Children* |
| AUTHOR: | Harris Clemes, Reynold Bean |
| PUBLISHER: | APOD Publications<br>1427 41st Avenue<br>Capitola, CA 95010 |
| MAJOR IDEAS: | A 33-page booklet of easy-to-use methods for setting rules at home and clearing up communications within families. There are excellent sections dealing with being consistent, fitting chores to the child, choosing effective consequences and rewarding good behavior, and examples of workable rules. The |

booklet is attractive, easy to understand and written in a very practical manner.

TITLE: *Raising Children's Self-Esteem**

MAJOR IDEAS: This 48-page booklet demonstrates how parents can help children become more self-confident, improve school performance, develop good values and attitudes, get along better with others and more. In addition, the authors (Bean and Clemes) give valuable advice for improving family life. The booklet is easy to read and understand.

TITLE: *Helping Your Teenage Student*

AUTHOR: Marvin Cohn

PUBLISHER: E. P. Dutton
2 Park Avenue
New York, NY 10016

MAJOR IDEAS: This guide gives parents the tools they need to help teenagers cope more successfully with the increased academic demands of today's junior and senior high schools. The author gives timely methods on what parents can do to help teenagers improve reading and study skills. Written primarily for parents of high school students, but possibly useful for parents of 7th and 8th grade students. (239 pp.)

TITLE: *FOOD: A Publication on Food and Nutrition*

PUBLISHER: U.S. Department of Agriculture
Science and Education Administration

For sale by: Supt. of Documents
U.S. Government Printing Office
Washington, DC 20402

MAJOR IDEAS: A series of publications by USDA that are designed to give up-to-date, reliable information about food and nutrition issues, and suggestions on how to apply this information to your food decisions. Includes articles, calorie charts, recipes, etc. Extremely attractive magazine, well designed, easy to read. (65 pp.)

TITLE: *Today's Family in Focus:* Eight illustrated pamphlets produced by the National PTA. Titles: (1) Parent Education, (2) Children's Rights and How Parents Can Protect Them, (3) Work and the American Family, (4) The Family in Today's Educational World, (5) Parents, Children and Preventive Medicine, (6) Children and Values, (7) Developing the Mind of the Child, (8) ABC's of Children's Social Development.

PUBLISHER: National Congress of Parents and Teachers
700 North Rush Street
Chicago, IL 60611

MAJOR IDEAS: The pamphlets are aimed at parents of elementary school children. Useful in parent education programs, as themes for PAC meetings or basic information for at-home reading. The booklets are attractive and contain helpful information on working with families.

TITLE: *Follow the Yellow Brick Roads*

PUBLISHER: Superintendent of Documents
U.S. Government Printing Office
Washington, DC 20402

MAJOR IDEAS: This 82-page catalog is actually a resource book containing career education ideas in four major sections: (1) Classroom, (2) Community Resources, (3) Counseling and Guidance and (4) Management. Each page is headed by a statement that expresses a career education idea and its relationship to a specific facet of education. Meaningful for parents and students. ($4.40)

TITLE: *Communicating with our Sons and Daughters*

AUTHOR: Marcos Behean Hernandez

| | |
|---|---|
| PUBLISHER: | Superintendent of Documents<br>U.S. Government Printing Office<br>Washington, DC 20402 |
| MAJOR IDEAS: | This 16-page, illustrated booklet examines the role of Mexican-American parents in the educational lives of their children. It is addressed to Chicano parents who are looking for ways to best prepare their children to meet the challenges of growing up and becoming adults in today's complex and sometimes confusing world. Written in an easy-to-read format. ($1.10) |
| TITLE: | *Look Out for Yourself; Helpful Hints for Selecting a School or College** |
| MAJOR IDEAS: | This 16-page booklet is designed to help parents and students ask the right questions to determine if the program or school they are considering is the best for them. It lists questions other students have found helpful in avoiding problems. It also lists additional sources of information to help with more specific questions. The booklet is well organized and easy to read. ($1) |
| TITLE: | *Caring About Kids* |
| PUBLISHER: | Public Inquiries<br>National Institute of Mental Health<br>5600 Fishers Lane<br>Rockville, MD 20858 |
| MAJOR IDEAS: | Illustrated pamphlets directed toward parents and teachers that describe what can be done to help children (and parents) who have these specific problems: "Helping the Hyperactive Child" and "Dyslexia." |
| TITLE: | *Inside My Mom — Dentro De Mi Mama* |
| PUBLISHER: | Supply Division<br>National Foundation March of Dimes<br>P.O. Box 2000<br>White Plains, NY 10602 |

MAJOR IDEAS: This filmstrip is targeted to high school students or parents with limited educational backgrounds. This entertaining and informative cartoon presentation approaches nutrition as the basic element of life. It is a natural lead-in for discussion about the basics of preventive health care. Also available in Spanish. (Produced as a filmstrip for a rental fee of about $10, or as a slide tape for about $15.)

PUBLISHER: National Education Association
1201 16th Street, N.W.
Washington, DC 20036

COMMENTS: This organization publishes filmstrips, books, leaflets and booklets on a variety of topics including parenting, motivation, helping your child to learn, discipline, etc. Write for a free catalog.

TITLE: *The Art of Parenting*

AUTHOR: Bill Wagonseller, Mary Burnett, Bernard Salzberg, Joe Burnett

PUBLISHER: Research Press Co.
2612 North Mattis
Champaign, IL 61820

MAJOR IDEAS: A series of five filmstrips and five parent manuals designed to provide parents with an understanding of their child's behavior patterns, and to assist them in devising techniques and methods for handling whatever problems arise. Specific attention is given to areas of communication, assertiveness and behavior management in a manner that will promote discussion and exploration of possible solutions, rather than promote the idea that there is only one way to handle a situation. (Purchase price: $125)

TITLE: *A Parent's Guide to Testing in the Schools*

PUBLISHER: Assessment and Measurement Program
Northwest Regional Educational Laboratory

710 S.W. 2nd Avenue
Portland, OR 97204

MAJOR IDEAS: The booklet identifies and answers some of the questions parents have about tests. It was prepared after consultation with parents in the Portland schools' Title I program.

TITLE: *Plain Talk About Children with Learning Disabilities*

PUBLISHER: Public Health Service
5600 Fishers Lane
Rockville, MD 20857

MAJOR IDEAS: The author explains who a learning disabled child is, why the child has this problem and how adults can help.

TITLE: *The Rights of Parents*

PUBLISHER: American Civil Liberties Union
Literature Department
132 West 43rd Street
New York, NY 10036

MAJOR IDEAS: The guide helps parents become aware of the rights they possess to protect themselves and their children from unnecessary and illegal action of the state. It includes chapters on such topics as Control and Discipline of Children, Education of Children, Parental Rights and Family Integrity, Separated and Divorced Parents, and Preventing Parenthood. In addition, appendices include an index of assistance organizations for parents and a list of uniform state laws on adoption, child custody, etc. Written in an easy-to-read, simple question-and-answer format. ($2.50)

TITLE: *The Confident Learner: Self-Esteem in Children*

PUBLISHER: Lawren Productions, Inc.
P.O. Box 666
Mendocino, CA 95460

MAJOR IDEAS: Principles for helping children develop self-esteem are stated while the camera follows relevant scenes in several classrooms. Targeted toward teachers and parents, the film stresses self-image and self-motivation (This 16mm color sound film would be ideal for parent education and teacher in-service training. It runs for 15 minutes.)

| | |
|---|---|
| TITLE: | *What Does a Reading Test Test?* |
| PUBLISHER: | Recruitment Leadership Training Institute<br>Administrative Services Building<br>Temple University<br>Philadelphia, PA 19122 |
| MAJOR IDEAS: | The authors of this 25-page booklet present test information and how it is graded and evaluated, and discuss the usefulness of test data. This material could be used as an effort to explain to parents how children will be (or have been) tested. Some technical words, but information is basically understandable. |

# Sample
# Parent Education
# Survey Forms

# PARENT INVOLVEMENT PROGRAM SURVEY

Name ———————————————— Phone ——————————

Address ——————————————————————————————

### Children in School(s)

Name of Child            Age      School

——————————————————————————————————

——————————————————————————————————

——————————————————————————————————

I would like to learn more about:

    ———— things I can do to help my child in school.

    ———— how to help in the school and classroom.

I would be interested in:

    ———— just getting to know more parents in the community.

    ———— being in a group that has fun and gets me out of the house.

    ———— craft classes.

    ———— learning more about what's going on in the community for me and my family.

If a group of parents got together, I would like to talk about:

    ———— ways to talk and listen to my children and work out problems.

    ———— ways to get my children to do what they need to do.

    ———— ways to manage so that my children get good food and health care.

    ———— ways to feel more comfortable talking with teachers, counselors, doctors, nurses . . . all the people who work with my children.

    ———— ways to deal with living in a community of many different cultures and a chance to learn more about each other.

    ———— ways to talk with my children about big things like life, death, love, sex, work, responsibility, education, money, trust, honesty, prejudice, drugs, alcohol, etc.

I could go to meetings: _____ in the morning.

_____ in the afternoon.

_____ in the evening.

_____ on weekends.


I think the best place for parents to get together is:

_____ in a home.

_____ at the school.

_____ community center/library.

_____ other: _____


Return this form to your child's teacher by _____

# THE INFORMATION YOU NEED

Bringing up children is not simple these days, mainly because the parenting job has many parts. Every parent feels okay about how he or she is doing on some parts . . . and every parent feels he or she could learn more about other parts.

This list tries to show you "the parts of the job of parenting" to give you a clearer idea of where your greatest interest is . . . and to give us a clearer idea of the best programs to plan. Thanks very much for taking the time to fill this out.

| THE PARTS OF THE PARENTING JOB | Hard for me | Sometimes hard | Easy for me | Could use more information | |
|---|---|---|---|---|---|
| a. provide good food and health care | ☐ | ☐ | ☐ | ☐ | (Circle the |
| b. see each child's strengths | ☐ | ☐ | ☐ | ☐ | three items you checked |
| c. know what to expect at different ages | ☐ | ☐ | ☐ | ☐ | here that |
| d. know how to help children learn | ☐ | ☐ | ☐ | ☐ | are most important |
| e. be clear about my values with my children | ☐ | ☐ | ☐ | ☐ | to you |
| f. be clear about me feelings with my children | ☐ | ☐ | ☐ | ☐ | right now.) |
| g. get children to do what I feel is important | ☐ | ☐ | ☐ | ☐ | |
| h. find good ways to work out problems | ☐ | ☐ | ☐ | ☐ | |
| i. get agreement among adults on what to do | ☐ | ☐ | ☐ | ☐ | |
| j. know how to talk about things that are hard to talk about (like love, sex, drugs) | ☐ | ☐ | ☐ | ☐ | |
| k. find ways to have fun as a family | ☐ | ☐ | ☐ | ☐ | |
| l. have good relationships with relatives and/or friends who are a real part of family life | ☐ | ☐ | ☐ | ☐ | |
| m. have good relationships with people who work with my children (like teachers, coaches, doctors) | ☐ | ☐ | ☐ | ☐ | |
| n. have workable relationships with neighbors and other people in the community | ☐ | ☐ | ☐ | ☐ | |

Name: _____  Phone: _____

Address: _____

# HOME-BASED INSTRUCTION BIBLIOGRAPHY

| | |
|---|---|
| TITLE: | *Teaching Young Children to Read at Home* |
| AUTHOR: | Wood Smethurst |
| PUBLISHER: | McGraw-Hill Book Company<br>New York, NY: 1975 |
| MAJOR IDEAS: | The author suggests that for some children home may be a good place to begin the highly individual process of learning to read and thus provides suggestions to parents about reading and preschoolers. Topics include: An Overview of Home Reading Instruction for Preschoolers, p. 3; What to Do If You Decide to Teach Your Child Beginning Reading at Home, p. 105; Teaching Beginning Reading Skills: A Step-by-Step Program You Can Follow at Home, p. 109. Appropriate for parents. (237 pp.; reading list for parents/teachers included.) |

| | |
|---|---|
| TITLE: | *Early Education: A Handbook of Teaching Ideas and Techniques* |
| AUTHOR: | Teacher Resource Library |
| PUBLISHER: | Macmillan Professional Magazines, Inc.<br>Greenwich, CT: 1976 |
| MAJOR IDEAS: | This handbook for early education is full of ideas for teaching colors, numbers and shapes, for stimulating language development and for making children excited about the written word, whether they are readers or pre-readers. All these ideas are integrated into broad curriculum areas and are firmly based in a philosophy that believes that children learn while living in their classroom, in their neighborhood, in their homes, in the whole, wide world. Topics included are: Things to Make, p. 32; Science, p. 41; Language Arts, p. 80; Reading Readiness, p. 88. Appropriate for staff and parents. (106 pp.; Bibliography included.) |

| | |
|---|---|
| TITLE: | *87 Ways to Help Your Child in School* |
| AUTHOR: | William H. Armstrong |
| PUBLISHER: | Barrons Educational Series<br>Great Neck, NY: 1961 |
| MAJOR IDEAS: | Provides simple practices (such as language exercises, working with colors) that can be used in the home to help the teacher and the child. Most suggestions are very old, but they are time-honored and in no sense obsolete. Appropriate for parents. (214 pp.; Bibliography included.) |

| | |
|---|---|
| TITLE: | *Early Childhood Education in the Home* |
| AUTHOR: | Elinor Tripato Massoglia |
| PUBLISHER: | Delmar Publishers<br>Albany, NY: 1977 |
| MAJOR IDEAS: | A book in which the author proposes a framework around which a new role can be developed—early childhood/adult educator. The book is addressed to all persons who deal in some way with parent and early childhood education. Contents include: Establishing Home-Based Objectives, p. 1; Creating Home-Based Programs, p. 22; The Home Visitor, p. 31; Developing Work Plans, p. 41; Administrative Planning and Operating, p. 56; Planning Workshops, p. 104; Viewing Human Development, p. 115; Developing a Record System, p. 255; Evaluation, p. 264. Appropriate for staff. (312 pp.; Bibliography included.) |

| | |
|---|---|
| TITLE: | *Helping Children Learn to Read, A Primer for Adults* |
| AUTHOR: | C. Thomas Pickering, Western Carolina University |
| PUBLISHER: | Chesford, Inc.<br>342 Madison Avenue, Suite 473<br>New York, NY 10017 |
| MAJOR IDEAS: | The author gives practical suggestions about reading for parents and teachers and special reading |

programs. Ideas about reading readiness, beginning reading, coordinating home and school instruction, etc. Includes book lists and word lists. (200 pp. 1977.)

# HOME-BASED INSTRUCTION RESOURCE MATERIALS

TITLE: *Tips for Parents*

PUBLISHER: Dallas (TX) Independent School District
3700 Ross Avenue
Dallas, TX 75204

MAJOR IDEAS: Illustrated paperback that includes activities and tips for those persons who work with children. It is published as part of a program called "Partners in Reading," 1977. The book can be used as a resource or guide to help parents plan activities for boosting the reading skills of children in grades K-3.


TITLE: *The Role of Parents as Teachers*

PUBLISHER: Recruitment Leadership Training Institute
Administrative Services Building
Temple University
Philadelphia, PA 19122

MAJOR IDEAS: Illustrated booklet provides specific activities that are designed for helping children at home. It is easy to read. Good for parents and primary teachers.


TITLE: *Helping With Reading at Home**

MAJOR IDEAS: Suggested reading activities that can be used effectively at home and/or at school. These activities are described in simple terms and can be presented to groups of parents who in turn can try them at home with their children. (27 pp.)

TITLE:       *Reading in the Family*

PUBLISHER:       State of North Carolina
North Carolina Department of Cultural Resources
Raleigh, NC 27611

MAJOR IDEAS:       10-minute color/sound film filled with ideas and
suggested activities for parents to use to strengthen
the reading skills of their children.


TITLE:       *Parent-Child-School Series*

PUBLISHER:       Moreno Educational Company
7050 Belle Glade Lane
San Diego, CA 92119

MAJOR IDEAS:       Four illustrated booklets written in Spanish and
English. (1) "Parents Learn How Children Grow," (2)
"Parents Teach Your Children to Learn," (3)
"Teaching Ideas for Parents to Use with Their
Children," (4) "Preventive Discipline and Positive
Rewards for Your Children." The main thrust of each
booklet is given in its title. They are useful for
presenting information at parent sessions. The
booklets are written in a simple, easy, step-by-step
manner.


TITLE:       *Parents and Students: Learn How to Study and
Improve Your Grades**

MAJOR IDEAS:       Illustrated booklet gives practical suggestions on
how a person can study and improve his/her grades.
Written in Spanish and English for parents and
students. (31 pp.)


TITLE:       *TV: The Family School*

PUBLISHER:       Avatar Press
P.O. Box 7727
Atlanta, GA 30357

MAJOR IDEAS:       Illustrated paperback of 63 pages. Anyone would find
this of interest. The authors (E. Morris and F.
Gregory) show how TV can be used to help educate
children. Games and other ideas are suggested.
Excellent for mini-workshop.

TITLE:        *Teaching Parents Teaching*

PUBLISHER:     Appleton, Century, Crofts
New Century Urban Education Series
New York, NY

MAJOR IDEAS:   This is a programmed guide containing specific
strategies for working with parents to teach them
how to work with their children. Positive
reinforcement is particularly stressed.

TITLE:        *School and After: Parents Help*

PUBLISHER:     Southwest Educational Development Laboratory
Austin, TX

MAJOR IDEAS:   Part of the Bilingual Early Childhood System, this
handbook discusses ways to involve parents in their
children's education. It is primarily directed to
kindergarten teachers. The home activities
supplements are related to the skills taught in the
bilingual kindergarten program.

TITLE:        *Children's Reading: What Parents Can Do To Help*

AUTHOR:       Richard D. Robinson

PUBLISHER:     Publications
206 Whitten Hall
University of Missouri
Columbia, MO 65201

MAJOR IDEAS:   This 20-page, illustrated booklet provides workable
suggestions for parents to help them create the best
atmosphere for developing their child's reading
skills. The author tells how to establish a home
reading program. He also gives 50 specific
suggestions for parents on helping their children
become better readers.

TITLE:        *Parent/Child Toy Lending Library*

PUBLISHER:     The JUDY Company
310 North Second Street
Minneapolis, MN 55401

MAJOR IDEAS:      A program for parents, teachers or volunteers to provide learning experiences that build specific skills in language development, problem solving, sensory awareness and fine motor coordination, and to provide content that builds self-image for the child, his family and his people. (Developed by the Far West Laboratory for Educational Research and Development.)

COMMENTS:      This is an eight-week course that can be operated by a local community person who need not have training in early childhood education.

TITLE:      *School and Home Work Together*

AUTHOR:      Harold Burks

PUBLISHER:      Instructional Materials and Equipment Distributors
1520 Cotner Avenue
Los Angeles, CA 90025

MAJOR IDEAS:      Targeted to teachers. Suggestions are given to help teachers work successfully with parents when children have specific learning problems.

TITLE:      *Helping Your Child Read at Home*

AUTHOR:      Abigail B. Calkin

PUBLISHER:      Oregon Model Center
Oregon College of Education
Monmouth, OR 97361

MAJOR IDEAS:      Illustrated, 8-page booklet that gives practical and simple suggestions for parents to help children build reading skills. Humorous illustrations. Very useful for helping parents find positive ways to work with their children.

TITLE:      *Johnny Still Can't Read—But You Can Help Him at Home*

AUTHOR:      Kathryn Diehl

PUBLISHER:      Cal Industries
76 Madison Avenue
New York, NY 10016

MAJOR IDEAS:     This 75-page booklet gives detailed instructions on how to help children with reading at home. Tips on the use of vowel sounds are given. Directed at parents and teachers.

TITLE:     *Who Me? Teach Reading?*

AUTHOR:     Kenneth Clouse, Dorothy Swan

PUBLISHER:     Kenneth E. Clouse
333 Quail Hollow Road
Felton, CA 95018

MAJOR IDEAS:     Filmstrip/cassette tape with guide (14 minutes) designed to help parents realize what an influence they have on their children's reading habits. This resource also has information that will "help parents to know what they can do to help their children succeed academically and how to do it." (Includes two booklets for use with parents.)

TITLE:     *How Parents Can Support Their Children's Learning*

PUBLISHER:     Project Follow Through
Bank Street College of Education
610 West 112th Street
New York, NY 10025

MAJOR IDEAS:     This booklet stresses the parent's continuing role in educating children as they grow up. It describes ways to reinforce education at home through cooking lessons, conversation, games and assistance with reading.

TITLE:     *Learning Is Fun: A Guide for Parents of Children Ages 4, 5, 6 and 7*

PUBLISHER:     Edisto Public Schools
Orangeburg School District 4
P.O. Drawer A
Cordova, SC

MAJOR IDEAS:     This handbook offers several exercises that parents can use at home to develop children's general learning skills and more specific skills in reading and math.

| | |
|---|---|
| TITLE: | *Parents and Children Share Experiences in Learning* |
| PUBLISHER: | Public School 243<br>The Weeksville School<br>Bank Street College Follow Through Program<br>District 16<br>Brooklyn, NY 11213 |
| MAJOR IDEAS: | This booklet discusses the goals and strategies of home-based instruction. It also offers specific ideas for instruction, such as games parents can play with their children and suggestions for organizing parental involvement in home teaching. |

| | |
|---|---|
| TITLE: | *Helping Your Child to Read* |
| AUTHOR: | Betty Jean Foust |
| PUBLISHER: | Division of Development<br>North Carolina Department of Public Instruction |
| MAJOR IDEAS: | This booklet suggests several learning exercises that parents can use with children before they enter school, during the early school years and when they become independent readers. |

| | |
|---|---|
| TITLE: | *A Family Affair: Education* |
| PUBLISHER: | The Home and School Institute, Inc.<br>1707 H Street, NW<br>Washington, DC 20006 |
| MAJOR IDEAS: | This book provides "recipes" for helping children learn at home. It also reviews much of the research on home-based instruction. ($10) |

| | |
|---|---|
| TITLE: | *The Three R's Plus** |
| MAJOR IDEAS: | This is a book of "recipes" for improving students' basic skills in reading, math and thinking, suitable for grades K through 8. ($12) |

TITLE: *Bright Idea**

MAJOR IDEAS: This book uses comics to provide ideas for helping families solve daily life problems. It shows how parents and children can create their own comics for instructional purposes. The book features an introduction by Art Buchwald. ($16)

TITLE: *Inexpensive and Easily Made Instructional Materials: A Training Manual for Teachers and Parents for Working with Preschool Children*

PUBLISHER: Casis Elementary School
(Early Childhood Program)
Austin, TX

MAJOR IDEAS: This booklet contains many standard kinds of activities that parents and teachers can do to help develop skills in preschool children.

TITLE: *A Catalog for Parents*

PUBLISHER: Developmental Learning Materials
7440 Natchez Ave.
Niles, IL 60648

MAJOR IDEAS: This 24-page booklet is a catalog of learning materials that can be purchased by parents or teachers to facilitate and encourage learning in children. These materials can be used in the home or at school.

TITLE: *Your Child and Reading: How You Can Help*
*Su Nino y La Lectura: Como Used Puede Ayudar*

PUBLISHER: Houghton-Mifflin
666 Miami Circle, N.E.
Atlanta, GA 30324
(plus other locations in TX, CA, IL, NJ)

MAJOR IDEAS: This 14-page booklet gives practical ideas on how parents can help their children with reading in the home. It includes a bibliography of selected books that can be used as starting points. (Available in English or Spanish.)

TITLE:      *Primer for Parents* (How Your Child Learns to Read)*

AUTHOR:      Paul McKee

MAJOR IDEAS:      This 30-page booklet gives fresh insight into how children learn to read. It uniquely puts parents into the position of finding out what it's like to be a child trying to learn for the first time. Explains the hows and whys of teaching reading to children.

SOURCE:      Edith Perry
Home/School Coordinator
Title I
Jackson Public Schools
1593 W. Capitol Street
Jackson, MS 39204

RESOURCE MATERIAL:      "How Can I Help My Children Do Better in School?"
"Math Tips for Parents—Parent Manual"
(Grades 4, 5, 6)
"Home Visit" (booklet before/during/after)
Letter to parents requesting their help and support in the Family Reading Project—a checklist of 12 ways to work with your child at home.

# INSTRUCTION AT SCHOOL BIBLIOGRAPHY

TITLE:      *Utilizing Teacher Aides in Differentiated Staffing*

AUTHOR:      Howard Brighton

PUBLISHER:      Pendell Publishing Co.
Midland, MI: 1972

MAJOR IDEAS:      A book designed to help develop the managerial skills of teachers charged with the responsibility of supervising aides in the classroom setting. Topics

discussed include: The Teacher-Aide Concept, p. 9;
Goals and Benefits of Teacher-Aide Programs, p. 41;
Legal Status and Responsibility of Teacher Aides,
p. 73; Program Initiation, p. 79; Classification of
Teacher Aides, p. 115; Selection, p. 149; Training,
p. 167; Utilizing the Aide, p. 185. Also provides
specific examples of Special Aide Usage on p. 213
Appropriate for staff. (247 pp.; Bibliography
included.)

| | |
|---|---|
| TITLE: | *Paraprofessionals in Education: A Study of the Training and Utilization of Paraprofessionals in U.S. Public School Systems Enrolling 5,000 or More Pupils* |
| AUTHOR: | Jorie Lester Mark |
| PUBLISHER: | Bank Street College of Education New York, NY: 1976 |
| MAJOR IDEAS: | A study that focuses on programming, training and utilization of paraprofessionals in the nation's school systems. The aim of the study was to fill a data gap in policy planning and decision making for future paraprofessional programming and funding. Appropriate for staff. (108 pp; Bibliography included.) |

| | |
|---|---|
| TITLE: | *Paraprofessional Work with Troubled Children* |
| AUTHOR: | James E. Gardner |
| PUBLISHER: | Gardner Press New York, NY: 1975 |
| MAJOR IDEAS: | This book is about an example of extensive use of paraprofessionals at the Children's Center for Educational Therapy in Venice, CA. The Children's Center has been heavily involved in projects using paraprofessionals since summer, 1966. It discusses the efficacy of using paraprofessionals in various settings and activities. Appropriate for staff and parents. (180 pp.; Bibliography included.) |

| | |
|---|---|
| TITLE: | *Practical School Volunteer and Teacher-Aide Programs* |
| AUTHOR: | Benjamin DaSilva and Richard D. Lucas |

| PUBLISHER: | Parker Publishing Co., Inc.<br>West Nyack, NY: 1974 |
|---|---|
| MAJOR IDEAS: | This book gives administrators and teachers practical guidance in planning and implementing volunteer and teacher-aide programs. It offers specific suggestions and ideas on recruiting, training and effective use of volunteers and teacher aides. Contents include: Establishing School Volunteer and Teacher-Aide Programs, p. 15; Training Volunteers and Teacher Aides, p. 35; Using Volunteers and Teacher Aides in Reading, Language Arts and Mathematics, p. 109; Volunteers and Aides Assisting in School Management, p. 123; Developing Volunteer Community Resources, p. 149; Recognizing and Evaluating Volunteer and Teacher-Aide Programs, p. 171; Appendix includes Sample Bylaws for a School Volunteer Program, p. 181. Appropriate for staff. (192 pp.) |

| TITLE: | *School Volunteers: What They Do, How They Do It* |
|---|---|
| AUTHOR: | Barbara Carter and Gloria Dapper |
| PUBLISHER: | Citation Press<br>New York, NY: 1972 |
| MAJOR IDEAS: | This is a handbook for volunteers who tutor. It gives tutoring tips, information about child and sample activities for tutoring reading and writing, new math, science and art. (Contents: e.g., the Role of the Volunteer, p. 13; General Tutoring Tips, p. 27; etc.) Appropriate for staff. (168 pp.; Bibliography included.) |

| TITLE: | *Parents and Volunteers in the Classroom:<br>A Handbook for Teachers* |
|---|---|
| AUTHOR: | Bette L. Miller and Ann L. Wilmshurst |
| PUBLISHER: | R and E Research Associates<br>San Francisco, CA: 1975 |
| MAJOR IDEAS: | A handbook written for teachers who wish to involve parents in their classroom program, but who don't |

know how to go about it. The authors share some of the attitudes found to be important when working with parents and provide suggestions for beginning a program which involves parents and other volunteers. Topics include: Recruiting, p. 7; The Community as a Resource, p. 19; Using Parents Effectively, p. 29, Making Volunteers Comfortable, p. 51; Planning, p. 67; Orientation, p. 77. Appropriate for staff. (135 pp.)

# INSTRUCTION AT SCHOOL
## RESOURCE MATERIALS

| | |
|---|---|
| TITLE: | *Teacher/Teacher Aide Roles, Relationships, Responsibilities* |
| AUTHOR: | Marilyn Seymann |
| PUBLISHER: | National Clearinghouse for Bilingual Education<br>1300 Wilson Blvd.<br>Suite B2-11<br>Rosslyn, VA 22209 |
| MAJOR IDEAS: | This 16-page booklet examines the role of the teacher and the teacher aide in the bilingual classroom. ($1.60) |

| | |
|---|---|
| TITLE: | *Confident Teaching: Enhancing the Self-Concept* |
| PUBLISHER: | Lawren Productions, Inc.<br>P.O. Box 666<br>Mendocino, CA 95460 |
| MAJOR IDEAS: | The main thrust of this 16mm color sound film (19 minutes) is the idea of enhancing the self-concept of students while stimulating learning. It is very useful for the orientation of new teachers, aides and administrators. (Rental fee: $40 per week.) |

| | |
|---|---|
| TITLE: | *How to Utilize Volunteers and Their Services* |
| AUTHOR: | June Baehr, Coordinator of Volunteer Activities |
| PUBLISHER: | St. Louis Public Schools<br>St. Louis, MO |

MAJOR IDEAS:   This handbook's suggestions of various ways to use volunteers and its suggestions for teachers who work with volunteers are particularly helpful.

TITLE:   *ABC'S: A Handbook for Educational Volunteers*

AUTHOR:   Jewel C. Chambers, Editor

PUBLISHER:   Washington Technical Institute
Washington, DC

MAJOR IDEAS:   A practical handbook with specific suggestions on interviewing volunteers, administering a volunteer program, recruiting volunteers, maintaining morale and so on.

TITLE:   *English Language Program for Children*

PUBLISHER:   Volunteer Service of Santa Cruz County, Inc.
Santa Cruz, CA

MAJOR IDEAS:   This is a handbook specifically for volunteer tutors. It contains many suggestions for oral language development.

TITLE:   *Parent Tutorial Program*

AUTHOR:   Linda J. Gulbrandsen, Parent Coordinator

PUBLISHER:   Boston Public Schools, Title VII
Boston, MA

MAJOR IDEAS:   This booklet describes how primarily Spanish-speaking parents became involved in the school.

TITLE:   *How to Initiate and Administer a Community Resource Volunteer Program*

PUBLISHER:   Minneapolis Public Schools
Minneapolis, MN

MAJOR IDEAS:   This is a guide to Minneapolis' experiences in setting up a volunteer program. Their community resource volunteers are people who present specific topics to classes. Especially helpful are the sample forms that they use for more efficient organization and recordkeeping. The guidelines for teachers and for volunteers are also good (they have special pamphlets for the teachers and the volunteers).

TITLE: *School Volunteers: Districts Recruit Aides to Meet Rising Costs, Student Needs*

PUBLISHER: National School Public Relations Association
Arlington, VA

MAJOR IDEAS: This is a good, practical guide for recruiting and training volunteers. It gives case studies as specific examples.

TITLE: *Manual for Volunteer Coordinators and Teachers Using Volunteer Tutors*

PUBLISHER: Des Moines Area Community College
Project MOTIVATE
Ankeny, IA

MAJOR IDEAS: This booklet describes ways to work with volunteers, and ways to orient them and the faculty to each other. It also outlines an orientation and training program. The sample forms are helpful.

TITLE: *School Volunteer Reading Reference Handbook*

AUTHOR: Charlotte Mergentime

PUBLISHER: School Volunteer Program
New York, NY

MAJOR IDEAS: This guide is used to train New York City volunteers to tutor in reading. Specific suggestions for reading activities on different word recognition skills are included.

TITLE: *Tutoring Resource Handbook for Teachers*

PUBLISHER: Superintendent of Public Instruction
Olympia, WA

MAJOR IDEAS: A guide for teachers who are working with volunteer reading tutors.

TITLE: *Administrator's Handbook for School Volunteer Programs*

AUTHOR: Harold D. Zier

PUBLISHER: Denver Public Schools
Denver, CO

MAJOR IDEAS: This handbook outlines the purpose of the Denver volunteer programs and the responsibilities of various school personnel—teachers are responsible for training classroom volunteers. Sample brochures, newsletters, etc., accompany the handbook.

TITLE: *Calling All Volunteers*

AUTHOR: J. Roehm, L. Vacanti and C. Hill

PUBLISHER: Central Printing
Tampa, FL

MAJOR IDEAS: A trainer's manual and a volunteer handbook to facilitate orientation to school rules and regulations covering the following topics which concentrate on the most common volunteer areas: reading aloud to children; tutoring individual children; playing games with children; sharing hobbies, skills and talents; listening to children read aloud; and helping with field trips.

TITLE: *Working in the Classroom*

AUTHOR: I. J. Gordon, P. P. Olmsted and T. Horms

PUBLISHER: Parents' Magazine Films, Inc.
New York, NY: 1978

MAJOR IDEAS: A set of five filmstrips that have as their titles: Parent as a Resource; Planning for Parent Participation; Training and Supervision; The Program in Progress; and Evaluating Parent Involvement. Also included are three audio cassettes and a discussion guide.

TITLE:               *Working With Volunteers: A Handbook for Teachers*

AUTHOR:        Bonnie Pinckney

PUBLISHER:     Tacoma Public Schools
                   Tacoma, WA

MAJOR IDEAS:   This handbook is designed to assist teachers in working with and understanding the role of the school volunteer. It discusses teacher responsibilities and tips for helping the volunteer feel comfortable in the school and in the classroom. (23 pp.)

TITLE:               *Volunteer Handbook**

AUTHOR:        Bonnie Pinckney

MAJOR IDEAS:   This 16-page handbook for volunteers is a companion to the handbook for teachers listed above. It describes the role of the volunteer in the school, discusses responsibilities, gives hints for working with children and answers questions that volunteers may have.

TITLE:               *Volunteers and Reading*

PUBLISHER:     North Carolina Department of Public Instruction
                   Division of Reading
                   Raleigh, NC

MAJOR IDEAS:   This 14-page booklet gives volunteers in reading some background information. It describes the benefits of volunteering to help students read, discusses tutoring techniques and lists suggested activities for classroom volunteers.

TITLE:               *Primary Reading Program:*
                   *Classroom Volunteer Coordination Handbook**

MAJOR IDEAS:   Designed for the school or district volunteer coordinator, this handbook contains workable suggestions for planning and implementing a program for classroom volunteers. It discusses assessment, recruitment, training, classroom management and the role of teachers and volunteers. (30 pp.)

TITLE: *How Parents Can Support Their Children's Learning*

PUBLISHER: Project Follow Through
Bank Street College of Education
610 West 112th Street
New York, NY 10025

MAJOR IDEAS: This booklet stresses the parent's continuing role in educating children as they grow up. It describes ways in which parents can get involved in classroom instruction, such as demonstrating crafts and skills and supporting individualized instruction.

# Sample Forms
# for Instruction
# at School

# REQUEST FOR VOLUNTEER SERVICES

| I feel I could: | SUBJECT OR AREA | TIME | DAY |
|---|---|---|---|
| Supervise small groups. | | | |
| Supervise individuals. | | | |
| Read to students. | | | |
| Check papers. | | | |
| Prepare materials. | | | |
| Set up audio-visual. | | | |
| Work in centers. | | | |
| Work in art classes. | | | |
| Work in music classes. | | | |
| Do drill with flashcards. | | | |
| Work in library. | | | |
| Supervise in cafeteria. | | | |
| Go on field trips. | | | |
| Help with clerical chores. | | | |
| Help on playground. | | | |
| Other: | | | |

Day or days I can help:        Hours I can help:

_____ Monday  
_____ Tuesday  
_____ Wednesday  
_____ Thursday  
_____ Friday  

_____

Parent's Name

Address

Telephone

Child's/Children's Name        Teacher's/Teachers' Name

Dear Parents,

We have had good response to our call for volunteer help, and now have a number of parents preparing material, running office machines and working with students.

But we still need "you" to help our children. If you have any free time that you could help at _____ School, call me at _____ or _____, or fill out the form below and send it to school with your child.

I will look forward to hearing from you.

Sincerely,

· · · · · · · · · · · · · · · · · · · · · · · · · · · · · · · · · · · · · · · · · · ·

Parent's Name _____

Child's Name _____

Homebase Teacher _____

Telephone _____

Day I Can Work _____

Time I Can Work _____

# REQUEST FOR
# CLASSROOM VOLUNTEER ASSISTANCE

Teacher: _____ Date of Request: _____

Grade: _____ Room: _____

I would like a classroom volunteer to help me with the following things:

_____ cutting and pasting materials

_____ mimeographing

_____ cleaning up the classroom

_____ helping class begin (by checking attendance, arranging the room, etc.)

_____ supervising children in the cafeteria

_____ putting up bulletin boards

_____ supervising children on a field trip

_____ supervising children on the playground

_____ general assistance such as taking children to the restroom, helping with snacks, collecting and filing papers and materials, translating for children who don't speak English, helping with audio-visual aides, etc.

_____ other: _____

I would like the volunteer to come on _____ (day) from _____ (time) to _____ (time).

Comments:

PLEASE SEND THIS REQUEST TO MRS. _____, PARENT COORDINATOR, AT LEAST ONE DAY BEFORE YOU NEED A VOLUNTEER'S HELP.

# QUESTIONS FOR TEACHERS ABOUT THE CLASSROOM VOLUNTEERS PROGRAM

1. List ways you have had classroom volunteers help you:

   _____    _____

   _____    _____

2. How often do you have classroom volunteers help you? _____

3. Do you feel the volunteers have been adequately trained to do the kinds of things you want? yes ___ no ___

4. In what areas do they need more participation? _____

   _____

5. Do you find you must spend more than 15 minutes planning for or explaining an activity to a volunteer? yes ___ no ___

6. If you answered "yes" to #5, do you mind spending this extra time? yes ___ no ___

7. Have you ever had to re-do a classroom volunteer's work? yes ___ no ___

   If you answered "yes," for which activity (or activities)? _____

   _____

8. Do you find that classroom volunteer assistance gives you more time to plan for and/or work with the children? yes ___ no ___

9. What suggestions do you have for the program? _____

   _____

   _____

10. Other comments: _____

    _____

    _____

11. What other activities would you like volunteers to be trained to do?

    _____

    _____

12. If you have reservations about a particular volunteer, please talk to me, Mrs. _____, parent coordinator.

# QUESTIONS FOR CLASSROOM VOLUNTEERS ABOUT THE PROGRAM

1. List the ways you have helped teachers:

   _____  _____  _____

   _____  _____  _____

2. About how often do you volunteer? _____

3. Do you feel you were trained well enough to do the kinds of activities teachers ask for? yes ___ no ___

4. In what activities or tasks do you think you need more preparation?

   _____

   _____

5. Do you usually have a good relationship with teachers?
   yes ___ no ___

6. Do you usually have a good relationship with the children?
   yes ___ no ___

7. If you answered "no" in #5 or #6, what kind of problems or misunderstandings have you had? _____

   _____

8. Do you enjoy being a classroom volunteer? yes ___ no ___

9. Do you feel that you are helping the teachers? yes ___ no ___

10. What suggestions do you have for the training? _____

    _____

    _____

11. What other kind of activities would you like to do in the classroom?

    _____

    _____

12. Other comments:_____

    _____

    _____

Note: If you have had a lot of problems with a specific teacher, please come talk to me about it. Mrs. _____, parent coordinator.

# VOLUNTEER'S SELF-INVENTORY *

Do I:

— make myself helpful by offering my services to the teacher when there is an obvious need for help?

— give the teacher adequate notice of absences by reporting them to the office before the day begins?

— realize that my whole purpose for being in the classroom is to assist the teacher in order that the students might progress more rapidly?

— avoid criticism of the students, teacher or school?

— have good communication with the teachers?

— try to maintain a friendly attitude toward all?

— accept criticism and suggestions without becoming emotionally upset?

— emphasize the times when students behave well and minimize the times when they fail to do so?

— plan for the activity that I have been assigned thoroughly, haphazardly or not at all?

— observe closely so as to know the individual student's likes, dislikes, preferences, enthusiasms, aversions, etc.

— find opportunities for giving students choices or do I tell them what to do at all times?

— really listen to what students have to say?

— give too much help to students rather than allowing them time to think?

— ask questions when I don't understand my assignment?

— evaluate myself at intervals?

*Taken from *Handbook for Volunteers,* School Development Project, Miami, FL.

# ADVISORY GROUPS
# BIBLIOGRAPHY

TITLE:      *Advisory Committees in Action*

AUTHOR:      Leslie H. Cochran, L. Allen Phelps and Linda Letwin Cochran

PUBLISHER:      Allyn and Bacon, Inc.
Boston, MA: 1980

MAJOR IDEAS:      This book provides a practical orientation to the implementation of the advisory committee concept. The book is based on the premise that before advisory committees will be used effectively, educational personnel need to understand the nature and function of advisory committees, to develop basic skills in using and organizing advisory committees and to have real examples and illustrations that may be adapted for advisory committee action. Topics include: The Development of Advisory Committees, p. 3; The Structure of Advisory Committees, p. 27; The Equipment, Facilities and Instructional Resource Review Function, p. 85; the Community Resource Coordination Function, p. 107; The Career Guidance and Placement Service Function, p. 131. Appropriate for staff. (336 pp., Bibliography included.)

TITLE:      *Citizen Participation in the Public Schools*

AUTHOR:      Robert H. Salisbury

PUBLISHER:      Lexington Books
D. C. Heath and Company
Lexington, MA: 1980

MAJOR IDEAS:      This book examines the practices and politics of local schools by focusing on the issue of participation—the possibilities and limits of active community involvement in the public school system. Topics of discussion include: Citizen Participation in the School, p. 21; The Community Contexts, p. 59; Who Takes Part in School Affairs?, p. 59;

Recruitment/Mobilization, p. 82; The Impact of
School Participation, p. 97; How Active Participants
Look at Their Schools, p. 163. Appropriate for staff.
(218 pp.)

| | |
|---|---|
| TITLE: | *The Politics of Education* |
| AUTHOR: | Jay D. Scribner, Editor |
| PUBLISHER: | The University of Chicago Press<br>Chicago, IL: 1977 |
| MAJOR IDEAS: | The purpose of this book is to suggest the politics of education as a relatively new field of disciplined inquiry and to present some of the current research efforts. Contributors to the volume include practitioners and scholars, educators and political scientists. Some of the topics addressed include: Participation, Representation and Control, p. 67; School Policy Culture and State Decentralization, p. 154; Education and Politics in Large Cities, 1950-1970, p. 188; Communication and Decision Making in American Public Education: A Longitudinal and Comparative Study, p. 218; Three Views of Change in Educational Politics, p. 255. Appropriate for staff. (367 pp.) |
| TITLE: | *Community Participation in Education* |
| AUTHOR: | Carl A. Grant |
| PUBLISHER: | Allyn and Bacon, Inc.<br>Boston, MA: 1979 |
| MAJOR IDEAS: | This book evolved from a conference on Community Participation in Education, sponsored by Teacher Corps Associates, which was held at the University of Wisconsin-Madison. The contributing authors addressed themselves to such issues as: Will schools change? How will they change? Who will determine the changes? The authors particularly focus on: historical perspectives of American education and of community participation; school budget, personnel and curriculum in relation to community |

participation; problems of community participation, past, present and those anticipated in the future; and proposals to effect viable community participation. Appropriate for staff. (262 pp.)

| | |
|---|---|
| TITLE: | *The Politics of Educational Governance: An Overview* |
| AUTHOR: | Harvey J. Tucker and L. Harmon Zeigler |
| PUBLISHER: | ERIC Clearinghouse on Educational Management Eugene, OR: 1980 |
| MAJOR IDEAS: | Why are experts and laymen dissatisfied with public schools in America? To what extent is the dissatisfaction unique to educational services? To what extent is the dissatisfaction part of a generalized negative perception of government? These are the questions explored in this particular book. They are explored within a historical and theoretical framework that emphasizes the inherent tension between experts and laymen regarding the political nature of educational governance in the schools. Relevant sections include: The Policy-Making Process in Local School Districts, p. 8; Recruitment of School Officials, p. 27; The Community and the Schools, p. 33; The Reform Movement and Educational Governance, p. 37. Appropriate for staff and parents. (67 pp.) |

| | |
|---|---|
| TITLE: | *Overcoming Barriers to School Council Effectiveness* |
| AUTHOR: | Jim Stanton and Ross Zerchykov |
| PUBLISHER: | Institute for Responsive Education Boston, MA: 1979 |
| MAJOR IDEAS: | This is a report on a year-long effort to support and evaluate local school advisory councils in five communities around the nation: San Diego, a suburban community in southern California; Fairfield and Calhoun counties in South Carolina; and Yonkers, NY. Interviews and discussions were held with school officials, state legislators, parents, and members of community organizations. Contents |

include: Field Strategies to Support and Evaluate School Councils, p. 38; Community Education Councils in a Southern California Suburb, p. 45; Networking Among Citizens' Organizations and Councils in South Carolina, p. 67; Barriers to the Participation of Hispanics in School Councils in Yonkers, p. 94; District Level Advisory Committees in San Diego, p. 106. Appropriate for staff and parents. (153 pp.)

# ADVISORY GROUPS RESOURCE MATERIALS

TITLE: *How to Conduct a Meeting*

PUBLISHER: Bakersfield City School District
Education Center
1300 Baker Street
Bakersfield, CA 93305

MAJOR IDEAS: A seven-page paper outlining the proper procedures for conducting a meeting. Includes sections on officer responsibilities, points of order and handling motions. Available in English and Spanish.

TITLE: *The HOW in Parliamentary Procedure*

PUBLISHER: Interstate Printers and Publishers, Inc.
Danville, IL 61832

MAJOR IDEAS: Illustrated, 56-page booklet presents a simplified form of parliamentary procedure. The booklet is well organized and the language is clear. It will help the chairperson and other officers to conduct more profitable meetings.

TITLE: *Organizing an Effective Parent Advisory Council*

PUBLISHER: National Coalition of ESEA Title I Parents
National Parent Center
1341 G Street, N.W., Suite 520
Washington, DC 20005

| | |
|---|---|
| MAJOR IDEAS: | A 65-page paperback handbook that gives information on how to organize and maintain effective PAC's. Further information is provided on PAC training, needs assessment, PAC goals and objectives, PAC election procedures, etc. Designed to give PAC's basic information on organizing PAC's at both the school and district levels. |

| | |
|---|---|
| TITLE: | *The Rights of Parents in the Education of Their Children* |
| PUBLISHER: | National Committee for Citizens in Education<br>Wilde Lake Village Green, Suite 410<br>Columbia, MD 21044 |
| MAJOR IDEAS: | The most popular book ever published by NCCE tells parents in plain terms what rights exist under law for them and their children. The book's goal is to help parents resolve educational conflicts without going to lawyers or resorting to lawsuits. Selected as one of the ten "must" books for 1979 by the American School Board Journal. (162 pp., $3.95) |

| | |
|---|---|
| TITLE: | *Developing Leadership for Parent/Citizen Groups** |
| MAJOR IDEAS: | What is "leadership"? How do you develop it in yourself and in others? How do you take the initiative? When do you assert yourself and when do you compromise? These and many other important questions about leadership development are addressed using school-oriented problems as examples. (60 pp., $2.50) |

| | |
|---|---|
| TITLE: | *Who Controls the Schools?** |
| MAJOR IDEAS: | Who has more power to decide how children should be educated: the school board, the school administration, teacher organizations, the courts, or the federal government? Do parents and students have any power? Should they? Hardhitting, far-reaching conclusions and recommendations. (76 pp. $2.50) |

| | |
|---|---|
| TITLE: | *Leadership: A State of Mind* |
| PUBLISHER: | National Congress of Parents and Teachers<br>700 N. Rush Street<br>Chicago, IL 60611 |
| MAJOR IDEAS: | Filmstrip/record set with guide. Gives good suggestions on developing or improving leadership skills. The materials may be used to help develop new leaders in the group or to strengthen the present advisory group leadership. |
| TITLE: | *Standard Procedures of Operation for Meetings; Rights and Responsibilities of the President, Vice President, Secretary, and Members* |
| PUBLISHER: | Migrant Education Service Center<br>3000 Market Street, N.E.<br>Suite 316<br>Salem, OR 97301 |
| MAJOR IDEAS: | Booklet discusses the procedures that should be used when conducting meetings. Includes a glossary of standard terms used in meetings, and a standard form for preparing an agenda. Written in English and Spanish. |
| TITLE: | *Planning Effective Meetings** |
| MAJOR IDEAS: | Companion booklet for above. Includes other vital points that make successful meetings. |
| TITLE: | *Working with the Bilingual Community* |
| PUBLISHER: | National Clearinghouse for Bilingual Education<br>1300 Wilson Blvd.<br>Suite B2-11<br>Rosslyn, VA 22209 |
| MAJOR IDEAS: | Anthology of papers discussing the importance of parent and community involvement in bilingual education programs. (90 pp., $4.50) |

TITLE: *Parental Participation in Bilingual Education**

AUTHOR: Alberto M. Ochoa

MAJOR IDEAS: Three approaches to involving parents in the decision-making process of the school or district.

TITLE: *Schools Where Parents Make a Difference*

AUTHOR: Don Davies, Editor

PUBLISHER: The Institute for Responsive Education
704 Commonwealth Avenue
Boston, MA 02215

MAJOR IDEAS: A collection of stories about schools in all parts of the country written by education writers and journalists. These schools are as far apart as Boston and Los Angeles, from urban schools in Minneapolis to schools on Indian reservations to a "dream school" in California. What they have in common are concerned, involved parents who support, help operate and shape their schools to meet the special needs of their own communities and children. ($3.95)

TITLE: *A Guide for Effective Leadership: A Parent's Handbook*

PUBLISHER: Clark College
c/o Johnnie R. Follins
Project Follow Through
Home-School Partnership Model
2945 Stone-Hogan Road Connector
Suite 200
Atlanta, GA 30331

MAJOR IDEAS: This 56-page handbook provides Follow Through parents with general and specific information that will aid them in participation at their child's school, at parent meetings and in the community.

| SOURCES: | RESOURCE MATERIALS: |
|---|---|
| Susan Gohmert, PAC Coordinator<br>Title I WISD<br>1601 Dripping Springs Rd.<br>Waco, TX 76704 | "Parent Advisory Councils—<br>　Linking School and Home"<br>"Parent Advisory Council Handbook"<br>"Ideas for Campus PAC Meetings" |
| Carol Merz<br>Title I Coordinator<br>Richland School District<br>615 Snow Street<br>Richland, WA 99352 | "A Handbook for Parent Advisory<br>　Councils" |
| Dave Fiscus<br>Sacramento City Unified SD<br>Consolidated Programs Section<br>P.O. Box 2271<br>Sacramento, CA 95810 | "Consolidated Programs Glossary"<br>"What Do Subcommittee Members Do?"<br>"A Guide for Advisory Committee<br>　Members—Staff Training Services" |
| Kim Kay<br>Educational Specialist<br>Oregon Department of Education<br>700 Pringle Parkway, SE<br>Salem, OR 97310 | "PAC Resource List"<br>"PAC News and Views" (Newsletter)<br>"Parent Advisory Councils in Oregon.<br>　Where Do You Fit?" (A Resource<br>　Book for Parents) |
| Edith Perry<br>Home/School Coordinator<br>Title I<br>Jackson Public Schools<br>1593 W. Capitol Street<br>Jackson, MS 39204 | "Purpose of Advisory Council"<br>"Handbook for Parent Advisory Council"<br>"Parent Advisory Councils" by Delores<br>　Lowe Friedman from Essence |
| Darlene Stevens<br>Title I Secretary<br>Spokane Public Schools<br>E 4714 - 8th Avenue<br>Spokane, WA 99206 | "Bylaws"<br>"Voting Procedures for Membership<br>　Election"<br>"Sample Voter's Registration Sheet"<br>"Report of School Visitation Committee" |

TITLE:     *School Budget: It's Your Money; It's Your Business*

AUTHOR:     Rhoda E. Dersh

PUBLISHER:     National Committee for Citizens in Education
Wilde Lake Village Green, Suite 410
Columbia, MD 21044

MAJOR IDEAS:     How to understand school budgets. What parents can do if they find irregularities in the budget. Where parents can get the necessary tools to personally analyze the budget. (192 pp. $4.95)

TITLE:     *Parent Advisory Council Handbook: Follow Through Program*

PUBLISHER:     Chattanooga Public Schools
Chattanooga, TN

MAJOR IDEAS:     This handbook discusses the various features of operating a parent advisory council. Included are sections which address organization and membership, selection of personnel, proposal and budget preparation, comprehensive services, staff development, agendas and meeting procedures.

TITLE:     *Keys to Community Involvement Series*

PUBLISHER:     Northwest Regional Educational Laboratory
Office of Marketing and Dissemination
710 S.W. Second Avenue
Portland, OR 97204

MAJOR IDEAS:     This series contains fifteen (15) booklets that may be purchased as a set or by individual titles. They are:

(a) *Community Groups: Keeping Them Alive and Well* by Greg Druian

(b) *Group Decision Making: Styles and Suggestions* by Greg Druian

(c) *Problem Solving: A Five-Step Model* by Susan Sayers

(d) *Planning for Change: Three Critical Elements* by Carolyn Hunter

(e) *Personal and Professional Development: An Individual Approach* by Susan Sayers

(f) *Governing Boards and Community Councils: Building Successful Partnership* by Diane Jones

(g) *Innovative Projects: Making Them Standard Practice* by Carleen Matthews

(h) *Successful Projects: Examining the Research* by Carleen Matthews

(i) *Effective Groups: Guidelines to Participants* by Susan Sayers

(j) *Group Progress: Recognizing and Removing Barriers* by Diane Jones

(k) *Measuring and Improving Group Effectiveness* by Diane Jones

(l) *Finding the "Right" Information: A Search Strategy* by Carolyn Hunter

(m) *Community Surveys: Grassroots Approaches* by Carolyn Hunter and Keats Garmen

(n) *Using Consultants: Getting What You Want* by Carleen Matthews

(o) *Group Leadership: Understanding, Guiding, and Sharing* by Greg Druian

TITLE:      *Citizen Action in Education*

PUBLISHER:      The Institute for Responsive Education
704 Commonwealth Avenue
Boston, MA 02215

MAJOR IDEAS:      This is the Institute for Responsive Education's quarterly journal of new models and ideas for citizen involvement in schools. It includes reports from Alaska to Florida on citizens and school people who want to increase citizen involvement in school decision making.

TITLE:          *Together: Schools and Communities**

AUTHOR:         Miriam Clasby and Joanne Lema

MAJOR IDEAS:    This is a handbook and resource directory developed
                from a project in Massachusetts to study and
                encourage school/community collaboration. It
                includes suggestions for advisory councils,
                organizations, and school and community people
                who are interested in "getting it together." (1975)

# Sample
# Advisory
# Group Forms

# SAMPLE FORM TO RECORD
# PARENT INVOLVEMENT

### Parent Involvement Report

School: _____ Grade/subject: _____

Teacher: _____ Date: _____

Parents involved                Activity

_____

_____

_____

_____

Use back of card for comments.

# EXAMPLE OF SPECIFIC DESCRIPTIONS OF PARENT RESPONSIBILITIES

*Fund-Raising Committee:*
This committee is responsible for planning, organizing and implementing fund-raising events for the year. Recommendations for events must be approved at the advisory group meeting.

*Social/Hospitality Committee:*
This committee organizes its members and other volunteers, who are not on the committee, to provide refreshments or food for program activities and events. Coordination with other committees is essential.

*Recruitment/Publicity Committee:*
This committee is responsible for the active recruitment of families into the program. It assists with preparing and distributing information sheets as well as in publicizing other program events and activities. It also organizes and implements the annual orientation of new kindergarten parents each June.

*Classroom Coordinators Committee:*
This committee acts as liaison between staff and parents, and as liaison between Executive Committee, committee chairpersons and parents. It assists and encourages each class and its teacher to select representatives for parent committees. Every effort shall be made to have an equal distribution of ethnic groups as officers and committee members.

*Site/Transportation Committee:*
This committee coordinates site evaluation and selection, if necessary, and assists in arranging bus transportation for students. It also monitors parent problems with the Transportation Department of the school district, working with school staff to document incidents. A co-chair is recommended for each school site. This committee should also periodically survey the parent group to assess whether there are recurring problems which the committee should address.

*Personnel Committee:*
This committee participates in the recruitment, interviewing and recommendation of new hires for the program. It also assists in the evaluation of staff. Personnel Committee meetings are closed meetings.

*Curriculum Committee:*
The committee discusses strengths and limitations of the curriculum, and assists in improvement implementation. It also helps in the review and selection of books for the program and helps in seeking out resource people.

*Political Action Committee:*
This committee promotes parent interests among school board members and school administrators.

# SUPPLEMENTARY RESOURCE MATERIAL FOR STAFF

TITLE:      *Putting It Together With Parents*

PUBLISHER:      Publication Sales
California State Department of Education
P.O. Box 271
Sacramento, CA 95802

MAJOR IDEAS:      This 12-page booklet is designed to serve as a guide for involving parents in the educational programs of their children. It is well designed and easy to read. ($.85)

TITLE:      *A Guide to Culture in the Classroom*

AUTHOR:      Muriel Saville-Troike

PUBLISHER:      National Clearinghouse for Bilingual Education
1300 Wilson Blvd., Suite B2-11
Rosslyn, VA 22209

MAJOR IDEAS:      For educators who want to know more about teaching in a cross-cultural classroom. (67 pp., $4.50)

TITLE:      *Follow Through: A Story of Educational Change*

PREPARED BY:      Nero and Associates, Inc.
208 S.W. Stark Street
Portland, OR 97204

PUBLISHER:      U.S. Dept. of HEW
Office of Education
Washington, DC

MAJOR IDEAS:      One of the chapters within this document addresses parent involvement (Chapter V). It discusses many of the mechanisms for facilitating parent involvement in the classroom and in the school.

TITLE: *Self-Assessment System for a Responsive Parent Involvement Program*

PUBLISHER: Far West Laboratory
Responsive Education Program
1855 Folsom Street
San Francisco, CA 94103

MAJOR IDEAS: This 20-page inventory can be used by anyone participating in or responsible for the involvement of parents in the education of children. Helps to evaluate the quality of a parent program, as well as determine areas in which changes might be made or new activities might be started.

TITLE: *Parent Involvement*

PUBLISHER: Superintendent of Public Instruction
c/o Gary P. Reul, M.Ed.
Old Capitol Bldg., FG-11
Olympia, WA 98504

MAJOR IDEAS: This 19-page guide is an ERIC list of resources for materials (books, journal articles, pamphlets, booklets) published on the subject of parent involvement. It is a handy reference for material that applies to both parents and administrators.

TITLE: *Language Development Resources for Bilingual/Bicultural Education* (051-1)

PUBLISHER: Dissemination and Assessment Center
for Bilingual Education
7703 N. Lamar Blvd.
Austin, TX 78752

MAJOR IDEAS: The aid to teachers of Mexican-American children features parent involvement information and activities and suggestions for activity centers: art, books, communication, discussion, games, listening, puppets, sensitivity, cooking and field trips. Bilingual resource materials include lists of books, films, filmstrips, community resource information and cultural awareness information. (English, some Spanish. Educators: grades K-3. Spiralbound, 243 pp. $4.50)

TITLE:                *Parents Organizing to Improve Schools*

PUBLISHER:            National Committee for Citizens in Education
                      Wilde Lake Village Green, Suite 410
                      Columbia, MD 21044

MAJOR IDEAS:          Step-by-step guide to organizing and running parent
                      groups in schools that can act effectively to upgrade
                      the quality of education and get parents into the
                      educational scene in a lasting way. (52 pp. $2.50)

COMMENTS:             NCCE has produced a series of five slide-tape
                      presentations based on Citizen Training Institutes.
                      Running time for each film is 12-15 minutes.
                      Individual filmstrips may be purchased for $27.50;
                      the full set of five for $110.

                      The five slide-tape presentations are:

                      *Organizing Parents and Developing Leadership*—
                      Illustrates how to build a power base among parents
                      and other citizens, run an organization and develop
                      effective leaders.

                      *Fund-Raising*—Illustrates how to seek and obtain
                      money from individuals, foundations and other
                      sources of funds.

                      *Parent Involvement in Collective Bargaining*—
                      Illustrates how the collective bargaining process
                      works, and how parents can make their voices heard
                      before, during and after negotiations.

                      *How to Work with School Officials*—Discusses how
                      to develop strategies for action, gathering facts and
                      taking the parents' case to school officials.

                      *The Law and Parents' Rights*—Shows how current
                      and proposed laws and court decisions affect
                      parents' and students' rights.

TITLE:                *Parental Involvement Handbook*

PUBLISHER:            Education Service Center
                      Region XIII
                      Austin, TX

| | |
|---|---|
| MAJOR IDEAS: | This handbook gives general suggestions for setting up a parent involvement program. One interesting suggestion is for a games-lending library. |

| | |
|---|---|
| TITLE: | *A Walk in Another Pair of Shoes* |
| MATERIALS AVAILABLE FROM: | Oregon Assoc. for Children with Learning Disabilities PSU Special Education Department P.O. Box 751 Portland, OR 97207 |
| MAJOR IDEAS: | 18½-minute audio-visual production emphasizes how it feels to be handicapped and how the normal child can be of assistance to a handicapped friend. The film slides are packed in a 140 size carousel tray and may be used on any slide projector that accepts a Kodak 140 carousel tray. Good learning and discussion tool for students, teachers and parents. (Rental fee: $5) |

| | |
|---|---|
| TITLE: | *Everybody Has a Song** |
| MAJOR IDEAS: | 20-minute filmstrip and cassette tape in which Henry Winkler gives a warm and sensitive performance in helping a learning disabled child understand why he is in a special education class and how he can benefit from it. The filmstrip also helps the learning disabled child believe he is a valuable person who can look forward to a fulfilling and productive future. (Rental fee: $5) |

| | |
|---|---|
| TITLE: | *Early Recognition of Learning Disabilities** |
| MAJOR IDEAS: | 16mm color sound film, 30 minutes, illustrates how many of the signs of learning disabilities can be detected by alert teachers and parents. The daily activities of children in kindergarten, first and second grade are shown. (Rental fee: $10) |

| | |
|---|---|
| TITLE: | *Resource Guide:* (For Vocational Educators and Planners); *Helping Displaced Homemakers Move from Housework to Paid Work Through Vocational Training.* |

| | |
|---|---|
| PUBLISHER: | Superintendent of Documents<br>U.S. Government Printing Office<br>Washington, DC 20402 |
| MAJOR IDEAS: | Shows how vocational programs can be extended or expanded for displaced homemakers in secondary or post-secondary vocational technical schools, community colleges, state universities, community-based agencies. (33 pp., $2.25) |
| RESOURCE: | *National Public Radio* (NPR) |

NPR is the national programming center and an interconnected system of more than 200 public radio stations across the country. Funded by the Corporation for Public Broadcasting and foundation support, NPR distributes approximately 45 hours of informational and cultural programming each week, including the award-winning *All Things Considered, Voices in the Wind, Pauline Frederick and Colleagues, Jazz Alive* and *Options in Education.*

*Options in Education* is co-produced by National Public Radio and the Institute for Educational Leadership of George Washington University. Principal support for the series is provided by the National Institute of Education. Additional funds are provided by Carnegie Corporation of New York and the Corporation for Public Broadcasting.

—Tapes and Transcripts Available—

Transcripts and cassettes of each *Options in Education* program are available at 50¢ per transcript and $5 per cassette. A brochure lists many of the special interest titles available in the series.

Many educators find that transcripts and cassettes are useful as teaching aids. Others use them in presentations to parent groups and in training programs for volunteers.

Subscriptions to *Options in Education* transcripts cost $20 per year. Forty-four new programs are produced each calendar year.

A program guide lists future topics planned for *Options in Education*. Transcripts and cassettes are available for these programs 10-14 days after their broadcast.

TITLE: *Follow the Yellow Brick Roads*

PUBLISHER: Superintendent of Documents
U.S. Government Printing Office
Washington, DC 20402

MAJOR IDEAS: This 82-page catalog contains career education ideas in four major sections: (1) classroom, (2) community resources, (3) counseling and guidance and (4) management. Each page is headed by a statement that expresses a career education idea and its relationship to a specific facet of education. Meaningful for parents and students. ($4.40)

TITLE: *Parent Education: The Contributions of Ira J. Gordon*

AUTHOR: P. P. Olmsted, R. I. Rubin, J. H. True and D. A. Revicki

PUBLISHER: Association for Childhood Education International
Washington, DC: 1980

MAJOR IDEAS: A monograph that describes the theoretical overview of parent education and involvement programs of Ira J. Gordon. Also included are descriptions and evidence of success of Gordon's six programs.

TITLE: *Parent Conferences in the Schools*

AUTHOR: Stuart Losen and Bert Diament

PUBLISHER: Allyn and Bacon, Inc.
470 Atlantic Avenue
Boston, MA 02210

MAJOR IDEAS: This book presents specific guidelines for working effectively with parents of children in the public schools. The emphasis is on the need to establish a co-equal partner relationship in order to provide early identification of children with special needs and develop programs to meet those needs as soon as possible. Discussions are included on the initial contact between school staff and parents, the evaluation process, follow-up phases, decision making, referral or special program placement stages, overcoming parent defensiveness, data collection, the use of school records, parents' rights under federal and state statutes, and alternative ways of avoiding adversary circumstances which arise from problem situations.

| | |
|---|---|
| TITLE: | *Annual Education Checkup Forms* |
| PUBLISHER: | National Committee for Citizens in Education<br>Wilde Lake Village Green, Suite 400<br>Columbia, MD 21044 |
| MAJOR IDEAS: | The National Committee for Citizens in Education has published a concise and uncomplicated form to follow and suggests that every parent conduct an annual checkup for each school-aged child before promotion time. The form shows how to review materials sent home by school, how to arrange and take part in a parent-teacher conference, and how to follow up. NCCE hopes that this kind of checkup will "help discover school problems early, and give parents and teachers a chance to work out a plan for each child to guarantee school success next year." |

| | |
|---|---|
| TITLE: | *Partners: Parents and Schools* |
| AUTHOR: | Ronald S. Brandt, Editor |
| PUBLISHER: | Association for Supervision and Curriculum Development<br>225 N. Washington Street<br>Alexandria, VA 22314 |

MAJOR IDEAS:   This booklet addresses this important topic. The authors review some of the premises and practices of parent participation; they analyze the assumptions, report on parents' perceptions of the curriculum and the school, examine the constitutional and legal basis of the parent role for power sharing, and suggest ways the relationship might be more productive. This document points out that parent participation influences student performance and that time spent with parents by school personnel results in better learning.

# Choosing Consultants for Training and Technical Assistance in Parental Involvement

## Introduction

This is a guide for choosing consultants to help you start or improve a parental involvement effort. Many individuals, small firms and larger agencies offer consultant services in parental involvement, including some funded by private or government sources and some that charge for their services or provide them at no charge. They may offer training (actual instruction) or technical assistance (advice), or both, in any of the functional areas.

This guide suggests a strategy for identifying prospective consultants and describes a procedure for screening them (i.e., for narrowing your list down to the consultant that seems best for you).

There is one task that you should complete *before* using this guide. You should first determine what specific consultant services you need and what resources you have available to support those services. The Self-Assessment Manual (SAM) can help you assess your needs. You can assess your resources by reviewing possible sources of funds and other support (e.g., private grants, government programs, civic organizations, district funds) and checking any regulations pertaining to your use of consultants.

The prior task is essential not only because you want consultant services to be as cost effective as possible, but also because you need to know exactly what you want and what you can afford before you look at the possible choices. Consultants vary widely in their educational philosophies, and the services they provide vary widely in type and intensity. Moreover, there are hundreds of consultants in the field of education; you can't possibly identify and screen them all. Thus, you will save yourself a lot of time and effort if you figure out exactly what you are looking for before you start looking.*

This guide is divided into four steps, which correspond to four sections of the accompanying Consultant Search Form. The guide offers suggestions for completing each step, and the form offers a set of specific questions to ask prospective consultants at each step. If you decide to use the form as is, we suggest that you keep this one as a master and duplicate the number of copies you need.

# Step 1: Identifying Prospective Consultants

Your first step is to assemble a list of consultants who may be able to meet your needs. We recommend the following procedures:

- Review consultants you have used in the past. They may be appropriate for your current needs or know of other possibilities.

- Check with consultants who led conferences you have attended or heard about. They, too, may be appropriate for you or know of other possibilities.

- Tell colleagues in your school or district what your needs and resources are, and ask them to recommend consultants they have used or know about.

- Check with local colleges to find out if any individuals or groups are available as consultants, such as people in departments of education and psychology or in a training center.

- Contact your state department of education and ask for names of possible consultants. The education department in your state may also provide some consultant services.

- Contact private organizations devoted to parental involvement.

Some of these sources may be suitable as consultants for you. But even those that aren't may be able to provide "leads" to other prospects. In some cases, you may backtrack a few times—from one source to

---

* Once you have chosen a consultant, you will also want to develop plans for what the consultant will do and when, and how you will evaluate the work. But these tasks, as well, are beyond the scope of this guide.

another—until you find several prospects that seem promising.

Section 1 of the Consultant Search Form (items 1-5) covers the important identifying information. It is often useful to record the source of the referral (item 5), in case you want to re-contact that source for more information about the consultant.

# Step 2: Getting References and Background Information

After you have assembled a list of prospective consultants, call or write each one to ask for references and background information. Get at least three references, preferably clients who have *recently used the consultant* and who had *needs similar to yours.* Useful background information should include a resumé describing qualifications and experience and/or a brochure describing services and philosophy.

At this step, you should briefly describe your plans. Some prospects will be able to tell you right then whether they can provide the services you need. Also, large agencies may provide many different services, so they will need some idea of your plans in order to send you the background information most relevant to you. Finally, telling prospects about your plans at this step gives them time to think about what services they would provide to meet your needs. Ask prospects to think about this ahead of time, so that if or when you call back, they will be ready to discuss details.

One more note: During this initial contact with consultants, some of them may be able to recommend others to add to your list of prospects (Step 1).

# Step 3: Contacting References

After examining background information on prospective consultants, you may want to talk directly with those that seem best suited to your needs. But, in most cases, it is a better idea to contact their references first. In relatively brief interviews with references (in person if that's convenient, but usually by phone), you can obtain additional information to help you lower the number of prospective consultants you eventually interview. Since interviews with prospects can be much more time-consuming, brief interviews with references beforehand can save you a lot of time later. Of course, if necessary, you can re-contact some references for more information after you have interviewed a prospect.

People are often skeptical of references, since many consultants will provide only those references who are their most satisfied customers. Usually you won't know whether there are other customers who were not fully satisfied. Thus, even after talking to three (or even more) references, you can't be absolutely sure that the consultant is right for you. On the other hand, if the consultant can't provide at least three favorable references, you have a good reason to cross that consultant off your list.

References are valuable for another purpose as well, not just for evaluating a consultant's work. By talking to people who have used the consultant before, you can find out how that consultant operates, what audiences (e.g., educational level or profession) the consultant works best with and what particular characteristics or quirks the consultant has that might affect your decision. These concerns are not necessarily relevant to the overall quality of the consultant's work, but they may help you determine whether the consultant is best for you.

Section 3 (items 8-21) of the Consultant Search Form suggests questions covering these points. We suggest that you duplicate this section as needed for multiple references.

## Step 4: Interviewing Prospective Consultants

The background information and references provided by each consultant will give you a good indication of which consultants are most suited to your needs. But before making a final decision, you will probably want to contact the best prospects for more detailed information. Schedule an interview with the contact person (item 1 or 4) or with someone to whom that person refers you. The interview can take place either on the phone or (and this is preferable) in person.

Section 4 of the Consultant Search Form (items 22-30) suggests some important questions concerning the consultant's availability, the services that are offered, the consultant's professional history, ways in which the consultant proposes to meet your needs, how much the service would cost and references for evaluating the consultant's work. Depending on your particular concerns, you may want to add some items to this section or delete others. But under ordinary circumstances, these items will provide a solid basis for a decision. Note: If possible, you may want to consider a "trial period," during which a consultant provides (and is paid for) some services before you make a final decision.

Item 28 asks which individual(s) would provide the services. If the consultant is actually an agency, you will want to know who would be assigned to you. That is especially true if you have been referred not to the agency itself but to a particular person in the agency. You may decide to request (or insist on) the services of that person.

The last item in Section 4 asks for the names of other prospective consultants. If you and/or the consultant decide during the interview that the consultant is not suitable (e.g., is too expensive or is not available when needed), you can ask for the names of others who might be. Even if you haven't decided whether to use the consultant or not, most people won't mind referring you to others whom you might also want to consider.

# Sample
# Consultant
# Search Form

# SAMPLE CONSULTANT SEARCH FORM

## Section 1: Identifying Prospective Consultants

1. Name:

2. Address:

3. Phone: (AC    )

4. If agency, name of contact person:

5. Source of referral:

## Section 2: Getting References and Background Information

6. Obtain names of at least three references.

   Name:

   Address:

   Phone:

   Type of Service Received:


   Name:

   Address:

   Phone:

   Type of Service Received:


   Name:

   Address:

   Phone:

   Type of Service Received:

7. Check materials received

____ Brochure

____ Resumé

____ Other (specify)

# Section 3: Contacting References

8. Name of reference (from item 6):

9. Has the reference used the consultant?

10. If so, when?

11. What were the reference's needs?

12. What was the audience?

13. What specific services did the consultant provide?

14. Were these services exactly what the reference expected and agreed to?

15. Did the consultant provide a clear estimate of cost *before* the services were provided?

16. How closely did the eventual cost match that estimate? (If the reference is reluctant to give actual figures, ask for a comparison of actual to estimated costs, using the scale below.)

| *Cost was more than 20% below the estimate* | *Cost was 6-20% below the estimate* | *Cost matched the estimate (within 5%)* | *Cost was 6-20% above the estimate* | *Cost was more than 20% above the estimate* |
| --- | --- | --- | --- | --- |

17. Did the consultant actively cooperate with the reference in defining goals and procedures for the services?

18. (If appropriate) Did the consultant offer training for the reference so that, in the future, the reference could provide similar services internally?

19. Did the consultant cooperate in setting up procedures for monitoring and evaluating the services? Or, did the consultant conduct independent monitoring/evaluation that suited the reference's needs and allow the reference to see the results?

20. Are there other aspects of the consultant's work or personality that were especially effective or not so effective?

21. How would the reference rate the overall quality of the consultant's work? (The scale below may be useful as a way of summarizing what the reference says.)

| Very poor (would not use again) | Poor (might use again if certain changes were made) | Adequate (would use again if no bettter consul- tant was available) | Good (would use again without reservation) | Very good (would use again whenever possible; services were superior) |
|---|---|---|---|---|

# Section 4: Interviewing Prospective Consultants

22. Record interview schedule.

Date:

Time:

Place (if in person):

23. Is the consultant available when and where needed? (If not, skip to 30).

A. Are you in the geographic range for consultant's services?

B. Can the consultant provide services on the days/times when you need them?

24. What services does the consultant provide (such as materials, ad hoc workshops, planned instruction units)?

25. How long has the consultant been working in the areas of parental involvement, both as a consultant and in other capacities?

26. Describe your needs and audience (type and intensity of training or technical assistance; educational and professional levels of audience).

27. How would the consultant meet your particular needs and handle your particular audience?

28. If consultant is an agency, specifically which individual(s) would provide the services?

29. What would the consultant's services cost?

30. Obtain names of other prospective consultants who may be available.

    Name:

    Address:

    Phone:


    Name:

    Address:

    Phone:


    Name:

    Address:

    Phone: